Words of Prai

Intensive Care for the N

"This book is a must read for anyone who is in the role of caregiver: nurses, doctors, home health aides, or anyone caring for a loved family member. Hueina Su has done an outstanding job of giving tools and techniques that are practical and highly valuable to caregivers. This book will inspire you as you hear her compassionate voice, giving you hope as well as solutions. Those reading this book can live their lives with deeper personal fulfillment and with more inner peace, ease and joy."

Terri Levine, Ph.D., MCC, The Guru of Coaching®, founder of Comprehensive Coaching U, author of *Coaching is for Everyone,* www.TerriLevine.com

"Hueina Su has written an excellent book for health care professionals, caregivers and all nurturers. As a public health care and patient advocate, I have worked with many doctors, nurses, cancer survivors and caregivers over the years. I have noticed that, all too often, we health care professionals don't always practice what we preach. As a result, we are very prone to stress and burnout. Hueina's book is a timely reminder for all of us to put our own health and well-being as a top priority, while we attempt to take care of our patients and loved ones. Through her personal story and coaching exercises, Hueina offers patients and caregivers inspiration, hope as well as practical tools for better self-care, joy and fulfillment."

Ming-der Chang, Ph.D., Vice President of Asian Initiatives, American Cancer Society Eastern, Division, www.Cancer.org

"We caregivers often hear the mantra, 'take care of yourself so you can take care of others.' I say that to others very often, yet until now I didn't really hear the message. Thankfully, I've listened to Hueina Su's wise words, *"intensive self-care is NOT being selfish and it's NOT a luxury"*. With her wise guidance in *Intensive Care for the Nurturer's Soul: 7 Keys to Nurture Yourself While Caring for Others*, I've been able to make some immediate and important changes. Self-care is a new path for me but I'm already less stressed, more balanced and on my way to becoming a better caregiver.

Connie Goldman, author of *The Gifts of Caregiving: Stories of Hardship, Hope and Healing*

"Wow! What a wonderful, useful and inspiring book. Although this book was written for caregivers, everyone who reads it will find useful tools to navigate through everyday life, work and family situations. As we move through life, we are all nurturers and caregivers for someone, in some way at some time. This book reminds us that we must not only provide care for others, we must also take excellent care of ourselves. This book provides simple and practical solutions, support and guidance for all kinds of nurturers - including you!"

Sue Urda, Co-Founder of Powerful You! Women's Network and Author of *Powerful Intentions ~ Everyday Gratitude,* www.PowerfulYou.com

"Hueina Su has written an exciting new book detailing a process by which overwhelmed people can reduce the stress in their lives and maintain a sense of balance. Called *Intensive Care for the Nurturer's Soul: 7 Keys to Nurture Yourself While Caring for Others*, Hueina's steps to personal fulfillment blend east-west philosophy with practical tips on managing multiple roles at work and at home. This is a must read for the 21st century."

George J. Juang, MD, FACC, Director of Electrophysiology Laboratory, New York Hospital Queens, New York Presbyterian Healthcare System

"Hueina Su has done an outstanding job in combining her Eastern philosophy, her personal experiences as a nurturer, and her excellent coaching skills into *Intensive Care for the Nurturer's Soul.* Through real-life stories and coaching exercises, she provides inspiration and personalized practical action steps to create a must read for caregivers and helping professionals."

Bruce D. Schneider, MCC, Founder and CEO of iPEC Coaching, author of *Energy Leadership:*

"In my work as a work & life expert for parents and as a mother myself, I've seen so many parents and caregivers suffer from stress and burnout due to lack of self-nurture. Hueina Su's book offers much-needed inspiration and practical strategies for all parents and caregivers to nurture themselves, so they can have more to give to their loved ones. She shares her personal journey with authenticity and compassion. It resonates with your soul, and gives you the permission and encouragement to honor and nurture your self."

Natalie Gahrmann, MA, PCC, CUCG, Author of *Succeeding as a Super Busy Parent*, www.superbusyparent.com

"*Intensive Care for the Nurturer's Soul* is an important book. We are all nurturers and caretakers in some way, shape or form. It is more obvious in times of crisis. Hueina Su provides both a loving and practical roadmap on how to care for ourselves while caring for others. The book is filled with valuable tools and techniques to help us avoid burnout and maintain balance during the most difficult times of our lives. We all can use the encouragement and direction that this book offers."

Alan Gettis, Ph.D., author of *Seven Times Down, Eight Times Up* and *The Happiness Solution:*

Finding Joy & Meaning In An Upside Down World,
www.DrGettis.com

"The world needs more advocates for intensive self-care like Hueina! The importance of self-nurturance is a powerful message that millions of women around the globe need to hear. Thanks to books like *Intensive Care for the Nurturer's Soul*, more and more women have the opportunity to transform their lives by receiving support for putting themselves and their emotional and physical well-being first!"

Renee Peterson Trudeau, author of *The Mother's Guide to Self-Renewal: How to Reclaim, Rejuvenate and Re-Balance Your Life* and president, Renee Trudeau & Associates, www.ReneeTrudeau.com

"As a recognized expert in the field of self-care for caregivers, Hueina Su writes eloquently about the need for caregivers to nurture themselves with the same commitment, passion, and soul that they nurture others. She offers practical advice, personal experience, and compelling reasons to make self-care a priority. This book is a fabulous contribution and one I will be enthusiastically sharing with my clients and colleagues."

Corrie Woods, author of *The Woman's Field Guide to Exceptional Living*, and women's self-care coach, www.womansfieldguide.com

"The love one shares with others starts from a seed of self-love and it grows endlessly to enrich others. Every day, parents instinctively nurture their children as all animals do. However, Hueina shows you how to extend the love towards work and caring for others outside of family. She introduces ways to first achieve inner happiness and therefore bring happiness to others. I feel this book is really a guide book for everyone who cares about others, a professor mentoring a student, a master guiding an apprentice, and surely a caregiver for a patient. This book should be an owner's manual for life."

Shih-Fen Chow, MD, Board of Advisors, American Cancer Society Eastern Division - Asian Initiative

"I felt like this book was meant for me. Hueina Su has captured the essence of a caretaker's role through her own experiences as an older sibling, nurse and mother. Her insightfulness sheds light on the relationships we take on in all the roles we play. This book is a must read for the caretakers of the world or who rely on caretakers to take care of their needs.

Hueina Su's ability to take a look at our own roles and how they play out in our relationships is the first step for change to occur. She continues to provide samplings of ways you can support that change for yourself to bring greater balance and substance into your life and into the lives that we live."

Linda Mitchell-Dominguez, Founder & Executive Director of Holistic Mentorship Network and MARCI magazine, www.HolisticMentorship Network.com

"Hueina Su speaks with an authentic voice about the struggles that nurturers face. Drawing from her years of practical experience, she has created an inspiring guide that gives us permission to care for ourselves as well as suggestions for the ways in which we can accomplish that."

Dawn Noble and Kathy Smyly Miller, Founders of Wellness Possibilities, www.WellnessPossibilities. com

"Intensive Care for the Nurturer's Soul fills a much-needed market niche. Caregivers will find the author's advice practical, yet heartfelt. She guides the reader with 'baby steps' that are achievable by anyone involved in caregiving. Caregivers will know instantly that Hueina Su understands them and the difficult journey they are traveling."

Christine Spear, Editor in Chief, Silk Purse Women magazine, www.SilkPurseWomen.com

"As both a caregiver and someone who worked in the medical profession for over two decades, Hueina's sage advice resonates deeply with me. *Intensive Care for the Nurturer's Soul* is a welcome lifeline for those of us who daily give so much of ourselves to others. Hueina's prescription for self-care is powerful medicine that will not only support us in nurturing ourselves, but will also help us to more fully honor and serve those for whom we care."

Ellen Britt, PA, Ed.D., Internet Marketing Strategist and Co-founder of Marketing Qi, www.MarketingQi.com

"Drawing on the rich cultural heritage of her Chinese family, Hueina Su artfully tells her story of love, family, relationships and the essence of the nurturer's soul.

By blending heartfelt anecdotes of her personal experiences, Hueina conveys her words of encouragement much the way you could imagine her caring for the most delicate patient.

By conveying a message of self-love, including exercises in recognizing one's needs, the author successfully brings her skills as a daughter, mother, nurse and certified life coach to the reader in a relaxed style that is sure to bring wisdom, strength and comfort to the reader."

René Cantwell, Founder, Families of Loved Ones magazine (strategies and resources for caregivers) www.FamiliesOfLovedOnes.com

"Hueina and I share a similar philosophy that self-care is not selfish, but serves the highest good of all. A healthy life offers a balance of give and take; of giving and receiving support. This is especially true to caregivers, parents, and anyone in a helping or healing profession. And yet many of us stumble on the "Yes, but how?" question. Hueina's book and experience provides a clear path for implementing this philosophy of self-care into practical steps, a pathway to balance and restoration. We can all benefit from her loving message, one that has the power to transform individual relationships as well as our society as a whole."

Karly Randolph Pitman, writer, speaker and founder of Firstourselves.com, author of *Heal Your Body Image: An Inspiring, Step-by-Step Guide to Loving Your Body, Overcoming Sugar Addiction,* and the upcoming *The Soul of Motherhood: Mothering our Children; Mothering Ourselves*

A gift for:

_____

From:

_____

Intensive Care for the

Nurturer's Soul

Intensive Care for the

Nurturer's Soul

7 Keys to Nurture Yourself

While Caring for Others

Hueina Su, MS, BSN, CEC

Ordering Information

Special discounts are available on quantity purchases by
corporations, nonprofit, universities, professional
associations, and others. For more information, please
contact customer service at www.RxForBalance.com.
Phone: (973) 664-0446
Fax: (866) 903-1442

Dedication

I dedicate this book to my parents Dr. & Mrs. Sheng-Chieh and Chang Chiao-Shing Su. Thank you, Mom and Dad, for always loving and nurturing me. I'm who I am today because of you.

Acknowledgments

I'd like to thank my husband C. Carey Yang for always loving, supporting, and believing in me. Thank you for loving me for who I am, and allowing me to continue to learn, grow, and transform myself. And most of all, thank you for dreaming with me.

A heart-felt thank-you to my mentor, friend and coach Terri Levine. Without your vision and encouragement, I wouldn't have been able to write this book and bring it to fruition. I extend my deepest and most sincere appreciation to you, Terri, for your guidance, support and for always believing in me.

A big hug and thank-you to my good friend Christina Genest for your help with editing this book. Thank you so much for your tireless patience, impeccable attention to details, and all your hard work. You helped me birth this book! I can't even begin to express what you and your continued support mean to me.

I'd like to thank my good friend Sarita Felder. Thank you for your friendship and your great input in the design process of the book cover. I so enjoy brainstorming with you, and appreciate having you in my life.

Thank you also to my good friend Lois Davis for helping me edit this book. You are always so caring and supportive. I appreciate your cheering for me over the years.

Special thank you to Becky Hannah for your wonderful proofreading and editing work, and to photographer Doug Zackers for my fabulous portraits.

Last but not least, a heart-felt thank-you and many hugs to my cousin Grace Liu. I'm grateful for your friendship, inspiration and love. You've always been one of my biggest fans. Thank you so much for being on this journey with me!

Table of Contents

Foreword

For more decades than I care to count, most of the stresses my family, clients, friends, and I encountered involved caring about someone or something too much, or needing care-giving. Hueina Su has beautifully birthed an idea that addresses the needs of caretakers of the world.

When Hueina asked if I would write her foreword it was an opportunity to look back on my life and reflect upon our first meeting, and what led to that for each of us. Like Hueina, my first career and passion was nursing. Nursing for me was and is a mixture of supportive, loving, compassionate care through troubles and a lot of coaching without necessarily calling it that. Extreme care-taking would be another term for the package that is nursing.

Care-taking spilled over to all other life activities for me. When I went on to become a holistic health educator, medical intuitive, psychic, animal communicator, and psychic detective (probably the most stressful of my work), I simply began taking care of others from my home or theirs. When filming for an A & E special, *Mediums*, (this show is still playing on TV around the world, yippee!), it was very important to me that the crew felt at home. The caretaker in me wanted to serve them all well and make sure we, as a team, were happy and comfortable with each other. One day, I noticed a limp and a grimace in one person, so I began asking and found that she was in pain and scheduled for surgery. I offered some help which she gratefully took. Caretaker at work with cameras waiting. One film crew for the *Psychic Detectives* documentaries told me I was voted the easiest in my category to work with.

My own life as a multi-tasking nurse, healer, educator, author, illustrator, psychic detective, wife, mother, grandmother and more is overflowing with things to accomplish. I strive to focus on caring for self and others at the same time. Not always easy with my life-long habits of putting others first. While I tell others to care for themselves, Hueina Su's book is the perfect gift to them and to me. Hueina epitomizes what I attempt to be, and that is one of many reasons why her book is long-waited help for me and other caregivers.

Hueina is, like myself, an adventurer who loves discovering new abilities. With her Black Belt in Tae Kwan

Do among many of her achievements, she appears to calmly glide through each task to tackle, each need to meet, each situation that comes her way, and meet the moment gladly and gracefully. She embodies what she writes about, and exudes peace that calms everyone around her. She is a beautiful Nurturer who also nurtures herself.

Since our first meeting through our dear friend, Christina Santiago, Hueina has become part of a wonderful team of healers helping others with aromatherapy as practiced in the French model. She added aromatherapy as an effective tool to help her coaching clients relieve stress, nurture themselves, and heal both emotionally and physically. With enthusiasm, quiet listening and much studying, Hueina quickly became an important fountain of knowledge in the subject for those around her. I've never seen her drained from her tasks at hand, whether it is her coaching, sharing healing information, or caring for her adorable children and her great husband, she truly embodies a model of taking care of self while caring for others. There is something so powerful about the ability to reinforce our own beliefs through reading and hearing someone so devoted to the need in all of us for self-care. That is why this book glows with truth and resonates so easily for all of us.

Our world is fast-paced and laced with a tremendous volume of constant information flow. The need to center ourselves, catch our breath and release the stress is probably more crucial than ever. How are we to accomplish this when we are faced with the overwhelming need to make a difference in others? Hueina's book comes at the perfect timing. *Intensive Care for the Nurturer's Soul* is a definitely gentle loving breeze with a clear and strong message effortlessly delivered. As I read her ideas, told in a wonderful story-telling style, it was easy to reinforce the truth that has motivated this book: caretakers need to take care of themselves. While we all know this, most of us (me included) don't always practice what we believe to be true. We need help and we need it in a way that is easy for us to use. Just read one small but potent piece to know why you will remember what Hueina tells us.

> " *Intensive Self-Care is NOT being selfish and it's NOT a luxury, but rather an essential practice for your survival and overall well-being.*"

It resonates with our souls. That simple, pure, loving statement brings me a sigh of relief. It is okay to re-prioritize, and for that and more I have gleaned as I read. I know that she has clearly embarked on a path to help us all continue our paths as healers while caring for ourselves -- the perfect mixture for a successful life.

In the light of love,

Nancy Orlen Weber, RN
Co-founder of the nonprofit Holistic Alliance International, nurse, holistic health educator, internationally renowned medical intuitive, speaker, and author of *Psychic Detective: True Stories and Exercises For The Soul,* www.NancyOrlenWeber.com

How to Use This Book

I wrote this book for all the Nurturers out there. From my years of coaching and counseling experiences, I share with you the top 7 keys to help you nurture yourself, while caring for others. In this book I share many of my stories as well as those of my clients. Please note that some of the names and personal information mentioned in this book have been changed to protect the privacy of my clients.

It is my hope that the stories, principles and strategies shared in this book will inspire and empower you to better nurture yourself, as you continue to care for others. Sometimes, just one idea can dramatically improve your life. However, it's not how many new ideas you can learn from this book that will change your life. **What will make a real difference is how many ideas you can put into *action* in your life.**

In coaching we always emphasize the importance of making a commitment, taking action and having accountability. At the end of each chapter I include a self-coaching session to further your learning and help you develop a few action steps to move toward your goals. There are also many resources on my website to further support you. I hope you will make a commitment today to take good care of yourself, and take action to create the life you truly deserve.

You are a Nurturer

To keep a lamp burning we have to keep putting oil in it.

-- Mother Teresa

Your Many Roles as a Nurturer

Chances are, if you are reading this book, you probably see yourself as a **Nurturer** in some way. Perhaps you are a professional Nurturer, such as a nurse, doctor, dentist, or other healthcare and holistic health professional. Perhaps you play a nurturing role in your career, such as a psychotherapist, social worker,

> **"There are only four kinds of people in this world: those who have been caregivers, those who currently are caregivers, those who will be caregivers, and those who will need caregivers." -- Rosalynn Carter**

teacher, nursing home staff, home health aide. Perhaps you are a Nurturer in your personal life, for example, a parent, grandparent, family caregiver, sister, friend, volunteer at a shelter, etc.

Only Four Kinds of People

Even if you are not caring for an aging parent, special needs child, or a family member who is ill, you could still be a caregiver. It's been estimated that only 10 to 20 percent of those requiring care in the U.S. receive it in institutions, which means family members or friends shoulder most of the caregiving tasks at home. In her book, *Helping Yourself Help Others*, Rosalynn Carter (wife of former president Jimmy Carter) stated, *"There are only four kinds of people in this world: those who have been caregivers, those who currently are caregivers, those who will be caregivers, and those who will need caregivers."* That pretty much covers *everyone* in the world! Mrs. Carter asserted that almost everyone has experience in caregiving, although the degree of involvement is different. For example, you may not be the primary caregiver for your aging parent, but you are still providing caregiving by calling or visiting to check in on them. Or, maybe your neighbor suddenly became ill and you brought her a meal or two to tide her over. Or, perhaps you regularly volunteer at nursing homes, soup kitchens, and/or shelters.

If you identify with one or more of the roles above, you are a Nurturer and this book is for you. As a professional life coach and wellness consultant, I work primarily with healthcare professionals and other Nurturers, helping them relieve stress, nurture themselves and create balance and peace in their lives. I teach my clients principles, skills and strategies of **Intensive Self-Care**, through one-on-one coaching, workshops and teleclasses, for example. This book is based on what I've been teaching my clients and my students over the years.

Delicate Yet Unbreakable

I chose Chinese plum blossoms as part of the design of the book cover because plum blossoms share some characteristics with Nurturers. Plum blossoms are the Chinese national flower. They look like cherry blossoms, except they bloom in the winter. The colder the winter is, the more beautifully they blossom. It is said that they were chosen as the national flower of China because of their resilience and perseverance.

> **As Nurturers, when we can cluster and support one another, we can become stronger and more beautiful -- as an individual and as a group.**

The delicate beauty, unbreakable resilience, and incredible inner strength of plum flowers remind me of

Nurturers. At the first glance they look alike, but, just like the snow flakes that fall upon them, each plum flower is uniquely beautiful. The flowers cluster to form a breath-taking "sea of flowers."

As Nurturers, when we can cluster and support one another, we can become stronger and more beautiful -- as an individual and as a group. Plum flowers may look delicate, but, they grow from a tree that's firmly and deeply rooted. Just like Nurturers, who are unwaveringly rooted... in love.

My Story

Destined to Nurture

I was destined to be a Nurturer. To tell you my story, I must tell you about my family. We have a long tradition of being professional Nurturers -- four generations to be exact. My great grandfather (my mom's grandfather), my grandfathers from both sides, my dad, several uncles and both of my brothers-in-law are medical doctors. My mom, my younger sister Phoebe and I are nurses. My youngest sister Gloria is a medical researcher. Three of our cousins are dentists. I wouldn't be surprised if one of our offspring goes into medicine or nursing in the future.

As I said, I was destined to be a Nurturer. Since childhood, I've had plenty of role models to learn from. My sisters and I were always playing "doctors and nurses". We lived in a small town in Taiwan. Our home was above Dad's clinic. I watched my parents take care of their patients every single day. Even when they were extremely tired, they were always kind and vigilant in their care for them. In fact, at times they were so focused on treating their patients that they neglected to take care of themselves. I remember Dad often missed his meals, worked way into the wee hours, and had to wake up in the middle of the night for emergencies. As an OB/GYN, it came with the territory. Because of his dedication, his patients all loved him and he is very proud of that. However, he hardly ever had time to relax or pursue any hobbies (and I know for a fact that he used to have many).

All Work, No Play

Dad always told me to work hard and you shouldn't play until all work is done. Since his work was almost never done, he hardly ever allowed himself to relax or have fun. As a child, I often wondered whether it was healthy to work so hard without proper rest and relaxation. My philosophy back then was more like "work hard, play hard". Of course, that didn't sit well with my dad. Now that I think about it, even as a young child I instinctively knew the importance of balancing work and play, and taking care of myself. Unbeknownst to me, a tiny seed was planted then for me to dedicate my career to share this message with the world.

A People-Pleaser was Born

As the eldest of three daughters, I was told to be the caretaker of everyone. I was told to let anyone younger than I to go first. I always had to share my toys and favorite foods with my younger sisters and cousins. If I showed any reluctance to share or take care of others first, I was told that I was selfish. My mom was always taking good care of *everyone* around her, sometimes to the point of sacrificing her own needs and well-being. My dad always said that mom is the role model for the three of us, but none of us is half as good as she is. I felt extremely guilty whenever I wanted to just relax, have some time for myself, or do what I enjoyed *first* instead of taking care of others or finishing all the work. For fear of being called selfish again, I overcompensated and became a people-pleaser, for which I paid a huge price in both my personal and professional relationships and career success. It wasn't until years after studying psychology and coaching that I was able to understand and modify my own self-defeating behaviors and underlying beliefs. Even now, I still catch myself. The difference is, instead of going down the old beaten path, I am now able to identify and quickly change my thoughts and behaviors, and choose the ones that support me.

My Epiphany

My epiphany came when we had just moved to Texas due to my husband's new job, and I had a home-based business then. My daughter was almost three and my son was around six months old. During our first winter there, both my son and daughter came down with bronchitis at the same time. They were simply miserable. Of course, being a good mother, I immediately took them to the pediatrician, received the diagnosis, got the prescriptions, and took care of them night and day. As you can imagine, it was no fun taking care of two sick children all by myself. With no family around, I was the only caretaker for them. It took them a couple of weeks to recover. In the meantime, I started coughing myself, and it got worse and worse. My chest hurt terribly. It felt like someone had punched me and knocked all the air out of me. I felt totally exhausted. However, I still forced myself to get out of bed every day to take care of my babies, especially my son whom I was still nursing at the time. I was so worried about my children that I totally overlooked my own symptoms. In the end, I coughed for more than a month until I recovered on my own. Believe it or not, it was then that I *finally* realized that I had been suffering from bronchitis, too! How could I have missed that?! I'm a nurse, for God's sake! And guess how much business I did in that month? Not much at all. I was barely surviving.

I learned a valuable lesson from that experience, and vowed never to do that again. It just goes to show you that doctors and nurses don't necessarily make the best patients, or follow their own advice. I realized the importance of taking good care of myself if I were to be a good wife, mother, and business owner. From my personal experiences and observations, I know that many medical professionals, moms, and caregivers have similar self-care challenges, either due to their caregiving responsibilities, limiting beliefs or negative self-talk that do not support their well-being. This is why I choose to dedicate my coaching practice to help the Nurturers relieve stress, create balance and nurture themselves. I firmly believe that whether you are trying to succeed as a caregiver

> I firmly believe that, whether you are trying to succeed as a caregiver or at your career, when you can effectively reduce stress and care for yourself, you will have more assets to succeed in your endeavors.

or at your career, when you can effectively reduce stress and care for yourself, you will have more assets to succeed in your endeavors.

Self-Care Deficiency Syndrome

A New Epidemic

It came to my attention a few years ago that more and more people are suffering from what I call *Self-Care Deficiency Syndrome*. I see it in my coaching clients, colleagues, business contacts, friends, family, and in many real-life stories I've heard and read. As a matter of fact, it's safe to argue that it has reached epidemic proportion.

We all need a certain level of self-care to maintain our physical, emotional and spiritual well-being. For example, we need sufficient sleep, healthy food, clean water, and preferably regular exercise to stay physically healthy. How about emotional and spiritual health? A supportive network of friends and family, satisfying career, spiritual practice and community, hobbies and other fun activities, opportunities to grow and utilize your gifts and talents, living a life aligned with your purpose and passion, are a few (but not all) factors that can help you maintain emotional and spiritual health.

In an ideal world, everyone would put self-care as one of their top priorities and be able to maintain physical, emotional and spiritual well-being most of the time. Sadly, in the frenzied, non-stop modern world, everyone (even young children) is under a tremendous amount of stress and there never seems to be enough time. When you are under stress, it's even more important to amp up your self-care practice to counter-balance the extra demands. The ironic reality is, if you are like most people, self-care is probably the first thing you let go when you are pressed for time. Over time, you will suffer from Self-Care Deficiency Syndrome.

Signs and Symptoms

So, what is Self-Care Deficiency Syndrome? Simply put, it's a collection of symptoms people display when they do not receive sufficient self-care. Some of the classic signs and symptoms are:

1) **Physical** -- frequent headaches, tension and/or pain in the neck, shoulder, back or other areas, digestive problems, racing heart rate, elevated blood pressure, difficulty falling sleep or sleeping too much, lost appetite or overeating, always feeling tired, frequent colds and flu, significant weight gain or weight loss, other minor or major physical dis-ease. When you ignore these physical signals your body is sending you, it has to "up the ante"

and send stronger signals to get your attention. **Research has repeatedly shown that chronic stress is linked to elevated risks of all major diseases such as heart disease, high blood pressure, diabetes, obesity and even cancer.** Many women skip their annual physical or mammogram, which could result in missed early diagnosis of a major illness.

2) **Mental** -- declined memory (not related to old age), loss of concentration, being forgetful, disorganized, absent-minded, feeling scattered and unable to stay productive, even tasks that were usually easy for you become difficult. You might procrastinate on tasks that you know are important, but feel too overwhelmed to do. These symptoms can cause decreased productivity, which in turn might cause more problems at work.

When you are under stress, it's even more important to amp up your self-care practice to counter-balance the extra demands. The ironic reality is, if you are like most people, self-care is probably the first thing you let go when you are pressed for time. Over time, you will suffer from Self-Care Deficiency Syndrome.

3) **Emotional** -- a general sense of unhappiness, feeling overwhelmed, depressed, hopeless, irritable, angry, resentful, feeling like a victim, losing temper easily, impatient, losing interest in things that you usually enjoy, withdrawing socially, anxiety attack, even clinical depression or nervous breakdown.

4) **Relationship** -- If you are a caregiver who lack self-care, you might feel drained from the caregiving relationship and even feel resentful toward the person(s) you are taking care of. If you are stressed from other sources such as work, you might damage your relationship at home because of the emotional symptoms described above.

5) **Unhealthy Coping Behaviors** -- such as smoking, drinking, drugs, emotional eating, temper tantrums, gambling, other addictive or self-destructive behaviors. All these behaviors can cause more problems in your physical and emotional health, relationships, work and/ or finance.

6) **Financial** -- If you engage in unhealthy coping behaviors mentioned above, get sick due to lack of self-care, or severely lose productivity at work, you can potentially suffer great financial loss as a result.

Are You an Unsuspecting Victim?

Let me ask you: How many of these symptoms do YOU have? When I present this in my workshops and classes, my audience often comes to a rude awakening that they have many of these symptoms. Many come to tell me that they didn't realize that they are already burned out, and they feel profound sadness that they have let themselves go to such extent. I always assure them that it's totally normal that they feel this way. And, it's totally understandable if you, too, feel this way.

First Step to Wellness

The good news is, self-awareness is the first step of any positive change. Now that you know you are suffering from *Self-Care Deficiency Syndrome*, and the long-term consequences you will face if you don't do anything about it, you can start making positive changes.

The great news is, from this book you will learn many principles, tips and strategies that will help you reduce stress, nurture yourself, create more joy, balance and inner peace in every area of your life.

From Self-Sacrifice
to Self-Love

Heal yourself first, before you heal others.
-- African Proverb

Mom's Advice

I remember vividly the day I told Mom that I was pregnant with my first child. My mom was overjoyed. This would be her very first grandchild and it meant the world to her. She congratulated me, and then she said something that stunned me. "Be prepared to give up at least ten years of

> **Intensive Self-Care Tip: Manage your energy level by taking mini energy breaks throughout the day, and on a weekly basis. Visit www.RxForBalance.com for a FREE Intensive Self-Care Kit, including the Intensive Self-Care Workbook, audio recording, and other bonus materials.**

your life for this baby." My first response was, "Sacrifice ten years?!! Um, how about me? How about *my* own life?"

Back then, I was approaching 30, loved my career, and had no intention of being a stay-at-home mom (although later on I did stay home for a few years and I would never trade anything for those years with my children). I know my mom was simply telling *her* truth. That's how she lives her life as a mother and wife. However, the concept of "sacrificing" ten or more years of my life was such a foreign idea to me that it shocked me, intellectually and emotionally, to the core. To me, this self-sacrifice parenting model sounds too "all or nothing." Even as inexperienced as I was, I knew instinctively that it's not good for my overall well-being. I remember thinking to myself, "Is this really the only way? Why can't I have my baby, my career AND my life?"

Self-Sacrifice as a Virtue

If you know anything about Chinese culture, you know that self-sacrifice is highly admirable, even expected, especially for women. Men are also expected to self-sacrifice, but usually only for a higher cause, like family honor, the emperor, or their country. The bottom line is, most people avoid being perceived as selfish at all costs, and they put their own happiness and self-worth at the mercy of others.

I was reminded of the virtue of self-sacrifice a few months ago when we installed satellite TV in order to watch Chinese programs. My ulterior motive was to spark an interest in Chinese language and culture in my children, by exposing them to Chinese TV programs. Well, the jury is still out on that one, but I did get some insights from the Chinese soap operas that I'd like to share with you.

My husband and I were watching this show about a group of young people who have complicated relationships -- you know, A loves B but B loves C, that sort of thing. Some of them are secretly loving someone, but wouldn't express their feelings, because they think "the other person" is better at providing happiness for the person they love, and therefore they should sacrifice themselves for the best interest of the one they love. Of course, there's all the guilt, should's, insecurity, shame, fears and regrets entangled with love. All of them act like they are not worthy of love, and their happiness and self-worth are entirely dependent on whether or not they receive the love from someone else.

"Oh, come on!!!," I exclaimed in disbelief, "This is the 21st Century! They are still showing this kind of story on TV??!!!" I was all wound up. My husband just shrugged.

After 20 years of living in the U.S., counseling and coaching countless people, I know that the Chinese are not the only group who think and behave in this way. The fact is, we are all more alike than different from each other.

Looking for Love in the Wrong Place

This reminds me of a story that Don Miguel Ruiz (author of "*The Four Agreements*") told in his book "*The Mastery of Love*." In the story, a man and a woman are in love. They love, respect and appreciate each other for who they really are. They have fun and enjoy their time together. There is no envy, jealousy, and no attempt to control or possess each other. Then one day, the man's heart is so full of love and joy that a miracle happens. When he looks at the beautiful night sky, he finds the brightest, most beautiful star. His love is so big that the star descends and lands on the palm of his hand. At that moment, his soul merges with the star. He is so happy that he can't wait to see the woman and put the star in her hand to prove his love for her.

However, when he puts the star in her hand, she feels a moment of doubt. This love is too overwhelming. The moment she feels this, the star falls from her hand, and breaks into a million little pieces. The man is heart-broken, and swears that love doesn't exist. The woman is heart-broken too, for she has lost the paradise she once had, due to a brief moment of doubt.

Who made the mistake? Don Miguel Ruiz argued the mistake was on the man's part, thinking he could give the woman his happiness (the star). The truth is, happiness can only come from

The truth is, happiness can only come from within us, not outside of us. You will never be happy unless you have enough love for yourself.

within us, not outside of us. The man and woman had been happy before because of the love inside of themselves. **As soon as he puts his star in her hand, he makes her responsible for his happiness, and nobody can be responsible for another person's happiness.** That's why she has the moment of doubt and breaks the star.

The truth is, you will never be happy unless you have enough love for yourself. Sadly, most of us are like the man in the story, trying to give our precious star to someone else, and desperately hoping they will love us back and make us happy.

Intensive Self-Care

Instead of looking outward for love, I invite you to practice *Intensive Self-Care*, which is an act of self-love. What is Intensive Self-Care? I define it as taking good care of yourself physically, mentally, emotionally and spiritually. It includes (but is not limited to) beliefs and behaviors such as loving and accepting yourself unconditionally, respecting yourself, honoring your own needs, having regular "Me Time" for yourself, doing the things you enjoy, eating a balanced diet, having enough sleep, exercising regularly, having annual physicals, enjoying quality relationships (family, friends, colleagues, life coach,

Intensive Self-Care is NOT being selfish and it's NOT a luxury, but rather an essential practice for your survival and overall well-being.

mentors) that support you, learning something new and exciting, managing your time according to your core values and priorities, knowing how to ask for what you want, asking for help when you need it, honoring and pursuing your dreams, knowing how to say "No," and standing up for yourself, etc.

Put on Your Own Oxygen Mask

Intensive Self-Care is NOT being selfish and it's NOT a luxury, but rather an essential practice for your survival and overall well-being. It's especially critical if you are in a nurturing role, either in your personal or professional life. It's like putting on your own oxygen mask FIRST before you help others put on theirs, when the plane hits turbulence in mid-air. You wouldn't be of much use to your loved ones if you didn't put on your own oxygen mask first and then passed out.

Research has repeatedly shown that chronic stress is linked to a host of physical and emotional symptoms and many major diseases. As a Nurturer, if you do not make a point to renew and recharge yourself, you will most likely end up stressed out, burned out, or having a physical and/or emotional breakdown. When you do, *everyone* you take care of will suffer with you.

> **As a Nurturer, if you do not make a point to renew and recharge yourself, you will most likely end up stressed out, burned out, or having a physical and/or emotional breakdown. When you do, *everyone* you take care of will suffer with you.**

Keys to My Success and Happiness

Over the years, as a mom of two, and having worked in many industries including nursing, counseling, coaching, education, nonprofit and small business, I have found that learning to practice Intensive Self-Care is one of the most important keys to my personal and professional success, life balance, and happiness. This is why I chose to dedicate my coaching practice in helping Nurturers learn the Intensive Self-Care principles and incorporate the self-care practices in their daily lives.

So, how do you practice Intensive Self-Care? First of all, get clear on your core values. What are your most important values and how are you honoring them in your life right now? In an ideal world, how would you like to nurture yourself physically, emotionally, spiritually? In reality, what does your self-care practice look like? Also

> As a Nurturer, if you do not make a point to renew and recharge yourself, you will most likely end up stressed out, burned out, or having a physical and/or emotional breakdown. When you do, *everyone* you take care of will suffer with you.

ask yourself, "What are my **non-negotiable self-care practices**?" These are the absolute MUSTS for you. For example, it could be reading, journaling, yoga, exercise, meditation, bubble bath, monthly girls' night out, yearly physical check-up, massage, manicure, or pursuing a hobby. It could be as simple as enjoying your favorite cup of tea each morning, or spending 15 minutes to just sit and breathe, or do nothing at all. It's YOUR choice.

Asking yourself these questions will give you clarity on what's important to you and show you the gap between your ideal and current self-care practices. **Please remember the purpose of this exercise is to bring awareness, NOT for you to judge yourself and beat yourself up for not taking better care of you.** Awareness is the first step to any positive changes. Once you have a good assessment of your current and ideal self-care practices, you can then design action steps toward better self-care and overall well-being.

If you are at the point of burnout, you might feel that there is an enormous gap between your current situation and your ideal self-care practice. You might even feel overwhelmed or hopeless about making any changes. Please know that it is totally normal to feel this way. A journey of a thousand miles begins with one step. **Take one**

baby step today and every day, and you will slowly but surely move toward wellness, peace and joy.

Take a few minutes now to answer the questions in the self-coaching section. They will help you gain clarity and take action today to start nurturing yourself on a regular basis.

Self-Coaching Session
Intensive Self-Care

✳ What are my 5 most important values? For example, family, faith, career, health, respect, freedom, creativity, altruism, etc.

✳ Am I honoring my needs, values and priorities? If not, what action steps can I take to change my current situation? Write down 1-3 baby steps you are committed to take this week.

✳ In an ideal world, how would I like to nurture myself physically, emotionally and spiritually?

✳ In reality, what am I doing on a regular basis for my physical, emotional and spiritual well-being?

✳ What are my **non-negotiable self-care practices?**

✳ Bridging the Gap -- If there is a gap between your ideal and current self-care practices, ask yourself, "What action steps am I willing to commit to take next week? Next month?" Be specific about what you are committed to do, and put a deadline on your action.

✳ What can I de-clutter from my schedule to make room for ME Time? Write down 3 things you can delete or delegate from your schedule.

✳ What resources (time, money, people, tools) do I have that could help me practice Intensive Self-Care?

✳ What support can I get from my family, friends, coworkers, or other help professionals?

✳ Write yourself an *Intensive Self-Care Permission Slip* -- Just as we write permission slips to allow our children to go on a field trip or participate in activities, you can write yourself a permission slip to practice Intensive Self-Care. Below is a sample Intensive Self-Care Permission Slip. Make as many copies as you like. Post it somewhere you can see daily as a visual reminder to take good care of YOU.

Intensive Self-Care Permission Slip

I hereby give _____
                    (fill in your name)

my permission to _____

_____

(fill in whatever self-care activity you choose,
including the date or how often you would like
to do it)

Your Name:

Your Signature:

Date:

Key #1

Stop, Drop and Roll Out of Overwhelm

The life of inner peace, being harmonious and without stress, is the easiest type of existence.
-- Norman Vincent Peale

Grace's Story

Grace started working with me a few years ago. She is a dentist who runs two thriving dental offices with her husband. She is a mom with two adorable children below age six (she had only one child when she started coaching with me), a devoted Sunday school teacher at her church, and a loving wife. She has an active social life with her friends and extended family. On top of that, she tries very hard to keep herself, her husband and her children healthy and happy. As you can imagine, it's no small feat for her to manage her life and balance everything. Together, we've worked on every aspect of her personal and professional life, and she has made huge improvements over the years. Of course, at times she still feels stressed when her life, her family, or her staff throws her a curve ball.

One time when she called me, she was overwhelmed by the constant bickering of her staff. "It's like I'm always trying to put out fires!" She said with a sigh. So we worked on some strategies she could use to communicate and mediate with her staff. She returned to work, armed with strategies and solutions to her challenge.

Fighting Fire With Fire

That night, my children and I watched a TV show together. A poor guy caught himself on fire. Frantic, he tried to run to the swimming pool nearby. I groaned, "Oh, no, he will never make it there!" My then 10-year-old son chimed in, "Yeah, everyone knows you should stop, drop and roll, NOT run!"

> Acknowledge your feelings of stress and being overwhelmed. This is important, since suppressed emotions don't go away. They only get buried in your body and will show up someday as a physical dis-ease.

He was right, *everyone* knows you should stop, drop and roll when you catch yourself on fire. You have most likely learned this life-saving principle in school too. But, when you are burning and panicking, it's hard to fight the urge to run for your life!

Overworked, Overbooked, Overwhelmed

That got me thinking. When my clients feel overwhelmed and stressed, they sometimes tell me that it feels like everything is burning, and they are on fire too. Their survival instinct is to try to "put out the fire" by

Intensive Self-Care Tip: **When feeling stressed, apply therapeutic-grade essential oils such as** *Peace and Calming, Stress Away* **and** *Tranquil* **to your temples, back of neck, wrists and other pulse points. Put some on your palms and inhale deeply for a few moments. Or, infuse your bath water with a few drops of these essential oils to melt the tension away. It's important to use pure therapeutic-grade essential oils, so you don't put more chemicals and toxins in your body which will cause more stress for your body. For more information on how to select and use therapeutic-grade essential oils, visit www.TrueHealingOils.com.**

frantically working harder and faster, trying to squeeze in more tasks in every hour, hoping to cross off more items from their ever-growing to-do list. They dive right in, bury themselves in the tasks, forego "non-essential" activity such as self-care and leisure time with friends and family... until they either successfully resolve the crisis, and/or run themselves down. **Rarely do I see people put out the fire without burning themselves in the process. If you have come down with a nasty flu or other illnesses after completing a major project -- you know what I'm talking about. Sometimes all you got from your frantic efforts was burnout and exhaustion.** As Abigail VanBuren so poignantly put it, *"People who fight fire with fire end up with ashes."*

Stop, Drop and Roll

So, what can you do instead? I suggest that you try my STOP, DROP and ROLL approach to reduce stress and get out of overwhelm.

1. STOP

When you are stressed and overwhelmed, stop, and take stock of the situation. Assess your stress level and stress response. Acknowledge your feelings of stress and being overwhelmed. This is important, since suppressed emotions don't go away. They only get buried in your body and will show up someday as a physical dis-ease.

Identify the source of your stress. Is it from external circumstances (such as job, relationship, finance, illness), or internal sources (such as unrealistic expectations or perfectionism)? Evaluate your situation carefully. What are the things you can control? What's out of your control? It's important to remember that when a situation involves people, the only person you can control is yourself. You cannot control the thoughts, beliefs and/or behaviors of anyone else, including your own spouse and children. What are you willing to let go and release in order to have peace?

Next, you need to set an intention. Instead of feeling stressed and overwhelmed, what do you intend to do, have and experience? Forget about the shoulds, musts and have-tos. What would YOU like to experience?

Take a few minutes to breathe deeply and center yourself. Oftentimes, when you are stressed, you feel

> **It's important to remember that when a situation involves people, the only person you can control is yourself. You cannot control the thoughts, beliefs and/or behaviors of anyone else, including your own spouse and children. What are you willing to let go and release, in order to have peace?**

scattered and cannot focus, which adds to even more stress because now you cannot think straight and cannot come up with a solution. Deep breathing exercises can help you lower your heart rate, blood pressure, oxygenate your brain, flush out the stress hormones in your system, so you can calmly assess your situation and tasks with a clear head.

It's also a good idea to take a break for Intensive Self-Care. Do something to pamper your body, mind and spirit. Or, go out and do something fun! You will come back much happier, lighter, and energized, ready to tackle your tasks.

2. DROP

Now that you are calm, take a look at your to-do list. I want you to use **The 3-D Principle (Do it, Delegate it, Dump it)** to assess each and every task on your list.

First of all, what can be dumped from your list? Pick out items on your to-do list that are not aligned with your intention, core values and priorities, and dump them from your list. Whatever is not important (by that I mean important for your long-term goals and well-being) and not urgent, dump it! Whatever you do just to please someone else, or do because you think you "should", dump it! These are the real "non-essential" activities that you can eliminate from your very full plate. Take a big red marker and cross them off your to-do list. I guarantee this will feel SO good!

Next, what are the tasks that can be done by someone other than you? Delegate those tasks. Don't worry about who will do these tasks for now. Just single out those tasks that you would like to delegate, and mark them on your to-do list.

What you are left with are the tasks that can only be done by you and you alone. These are tasks that are important to you, and aligned with your intention, core values and priorities. Number these tasks on your list according to priorities. Now you are ready to move to the next step.

3. ROLL

Now that you have pared down your to-do list, let's **roll out an action plan** to get things done! Go to the number one (the most important) task on your list. Determine what specific action you need to take to accomplish this task and how much time each action takes.

Often, there is more than one action step for each task, and you might underestimate how much time you actually need to prepare and complete the task. The result is that you either overlook things that need to be done or prepared in advance, can't get started because you don't have everything ready, or can't finish the task because you run out of time. Of course, this will create more stress and overwhelm. I suggest you break down each task on your to-do list to the smallest action step possible. This will give you a flowchart of action steps and a more accurate estimate of time needed to complete each task. Once you have all the action steps determined and know how much time you need, plug them into your calendar. When you finish planning the first item on your list, keep going down the list until you are done.

For the items that you'd like to delegate to others, specify who will be doing each task. Ask yourself: "What resources (people, money, time, tools, etc.) do I need to accomplish this task?" Perhaps your coworkers or assistant can help you with certain tasks at work. Perhaps your husband can take your place in giving your child a bath, walking the dog, or feeding your elderly father. Perhaps your children can pitch in and help with housework and yard work.

Sometimes you might benefit from hiring help, such as a professional life coach, accountant, professional organizer, in-home health aide, visiting nurse, personal trainer, or virtual assistant. There are also many other helpful services that can reduce your workload and make your life easier. For example, there are people who can run your errands, walk your dog, deliver your groceries, take your parent to doctors' appointments and renew your driver's license. You can also hire your neighborhood teenagers to do many things such as baby-sitting, yard work, and administrative work.

Be creative. Sometimes you can find help without spending out-of-pocket money. Years ago when my children were little, I used to swap childcare with my friends and neighbors. It saved us money and my husband and I went out feeling assured that our children were cared for by someone we knew and trusted. Sometimes you can exchange tasks you don't like with someone who happens to enjoy (or at least wouldn't mind) doing them. My good friend Heather shared this tip with me awhile ago. When

> **Sometimes things don't work out the way you want, because there is a bigger plan for you that you are unaware of. You are on the right journey, even when you encounter what might appear to be setbacks, heartbreaks, disappointments, or unnecessary detours. Perhaps you are meant to learn an important lesson, or perhaps there is a blessing in disguise.**

her boys were little, she used to have weekly play dates with a friend who also had young children. While their boys played, she would clean her friend's house, while her friend cooked a few meals for her to bring home. Their children always had a great time, and they both got their tasks done. I thought that was ingenious.

Occasionally, things don't go as planned. In order to achieve your goal without stressing yourself out, you need to be willing to **roll with the punches**. My yoga teacher Julia always says, *"Balance and flexibility prevents injury."* She was referring to sports injury, but the same principle applies to life. Be flexible about how things get done. When you are totally open and detached from the outcome, sometimes things work out in a way that you would never have imagined.

The Thanksgiving Sushi

This Thanksgiving, I set an intention to have a joyful, fun-filled holiday that's also effortless. I wanted to enjoy spending time with my family while having some time to myself. I love cooking, but laboring in the kitchen for hours to cook something I'm not that crazy about, just doesn't interest me. In an attempt to simplify my holiday tasks, I tried to sell my children the concept of Thanksgiving Sushi. I figure, we all love sushi and I really don't have much attachment to a traditional turkey dinner.

Why not? Well, as it turned out, my children were actually looking forward to a traditional Thanksgiving dinner. When I offered sushi, they decided that they wanted both! So, instead of simplifying our Thanksgiving menu, they were suggesting "doubling" it. Being flexible, accommodating, yet sticking to my original intention of an effortless Thanksgiving, I offered to let them choose one of the two. Together, we decided to

> Be flexible about how things get done. When you are totally open and detached from the outcome, sometimes things work out in a way that you would never have imagined.

order a traditional turkey dinner from a store. We'd have turkey, and I wouldn't have to cook. Then, something unexpected happened.

The day before Thanksgiving, I got a call from my little sister, asking me if we had any plans for Thanksgiving. Her in-laws were coming to her house for Thanksgiving, and my brother-in-law wanted to invite us too. I happily obliged and we brought a side dish to join the party. As I was helping my sister get her side dishes ready, she told me that her in-laws were going to bring some food for dinner, but she didn't know what exactly they would bring besides a turkey. Neither of us expected the feast they brought. Besides a huge golden roasted turkey, they walked in with Peking duck, crabs, lobsters and fish. I was overjoyed to see all my favorite seafood! We had an absolute blast with my sister's family and her in-laws. I got my wish and so much more, all because I was willing to be open and go with the flow.

If, despite your best intention and best efforts, things just don't go your way, let it **roll off your shoulder**. One of my favorite quotes from Dr. Wayne Dyer is, *"Have a mind that is open to everything, and attached to nothing."* I believe that everything happens for a reason. There are no accidents. Sometimes things don't work out the way you want because there is a bigger plan for you that you are unaware of. You are on the right journey, even when you encounter what might appear to be setbacks, heartbreaks,

> **Sometimes things don't work out the way you want because there is a bigger plan for you that you are unaware of. You are on the right journey, even when you encounter what might appear to be setbacks, heartbreaks, disappointments, or unnecessary detours. Perhaps you are meant to learn an important lesson, or perhaps there is a blessing in disguise.**

disappointments, or unnecessary detours. Perhaps you are meant to learn an important lesson, or perhaps there is a blessing in disguise. Think about the men (or women) you are so glad you didn't marry years ago, or the "dream job" you thought you wanted so badly and now you can clearly see how miserable you would be if you had gotten it. In my own life and in my years of counseling and coaching clients, I've seen countless such examples. I've heard it over and over again, "I thought that was the *worst* thing that could happen to me, now I can see that it was actually a blessing in disguise." If you choose to trust that the Universe always has your best interests in mind and everything happens for a reason, you will remain peaceful despite the chaos around you.

Self-Coaching Session
Stop, Drop and Roll Out of Overwhelm

* Self-assessment: Are you stressed and overwhelmed right now? On a scale of 1 to 10, 1 being completely calm and relaxed, and 10 being completely overwhelmed, where are you on the scale?

* What's your stress response? Refer to the previous chapter of *Self-Care Deficiency Syndrome*, and jot down the signs and symptoms of stress you are experiencing here.

* Take an Intensive Self-Care break. Do something that nurtures you and makes your heart sing. Write down 1 or 2 things you can do right now to quickly calm yourself.

* Set your intention: Instead of feeling stressed and overwhelmed, what do you intend to experience?

✳ Where does your stress come from? List both external and internal factors that stress you out.

✳ Identify the "internal stressors" as well as the factors that you *cannot* control. Ask yourself, "What am I willing to do to release them, so that I can have peace and calm?" Jot down your answer here.

✳ Now, cross out the items on your list that you *cannot* control. You are left with the items you can take action on (your Action List).

✳ Using the 3-D Principle, cross out the items you would like to dump from your Action List. With colored pens or markers, mark the rest with either Do or Delegate.

* Now you are ready to roll out your action plan. Devise action steps for each item that's still left on your Action List. Plug each action step on your calendar.

Key #2

De-Clutter for Inner Peace

If you let go a little you will have a little peace;
if you let go a lot you will have a lot of peace;
if you let go completely you will have complete peace.
-- Ajahn Chah, 1918-1992, Thai Meditation Master

An Empty Desk

Earlier this year, in an attempt to streamline and simplify my life, I hired Carla, a professional organizer. We started from my closet, and worked through my living room, home office and garage. Next we will be tackling my kitchen. The de-cluttering process proved to be exhilarating and enlightening.

I admit I've never been a perfectly organized person. It runs in my family. One of my sisters once joked that her whole family are pack rats. My own style is more like "organized clutter." On the surface, my space is cluttered, but I pretty much know where my stuff is. My excuse is, I'm a very creative person. Need I say more? I never understand how people could keep a desk that's virtually empty. I once heard someone say, *"If a cluttered desk is the sign of a cluttered mind, what is the significance of an empty desk?"* If you also have a less-than-perfectly-organized desk, you'll probably take comfort in this quote.

Even though I think I'm functioning well in my space, I've got to admit, sometimes the sight of the clutter distracts or even irritates me. With Carla's help, my husband and I donated tons of clothes, shoes, toys, books, and other household items that were just collecting dust and cluttering our home. I'm especially proud of our accomplishment of clearing and organizing our garage. We used to have boxes of stuff from the last time we moved, which was eight years ago. At the end of the long, hard-working afternoon, we stood in our garage in amazement -- there's so much space.

One of the many things I learned from Carla is, **organize your life according to how you live *right now* -- not how you used to or how you think you might in the future.** I found that I was holding on to many clothes from years ago, only because they were gifts from my parents. Now that I had a chance to review them and acknowledge that I will never wear them again, I gladly gave up my prized possessions, taking comfort that someone else will be able to enjoy them. I felt so much lighter.

Emotional Clutter

In my years of counseling and coaching experiences, I've found that many of my clients also have clutter challenges, and some of them are professional organizers and coaches. Yes, it can happen to the best of us. **While clutter and disorganization at work or at home can negatively affect productivity and relationships (many couples fight over this issue), I've found that emotional clutter is even more detrimental to one's success and well-being. It's the root cause of many people's stress.** Below is a list of many common emotional clutter issues.

Ghosts from the Past

Some people hold on to resentment, anger, guilt, and hurt from their past. Have you ever seen older people with permanently grouchy faces? It's like they are wearing years of pain, hurt and resentment on their faces, and they tend to see the not-so-perfect quality in everyone around them. Maybe someone wronged them in the past, and they still feel resentful and wouldn't forgive that person. Maybe they feel guilty for what they did or did not do years ago, and still beat themselves up over and over. Resentment and guilt can ruin any relationship. Have you ever tried to guilt trip someone? How effective is that? If you are in a relationship with someone who tries to make you feel guilty, I bet you would feel resentful toward that person over time. Malachy McCourt once said, *"Resentment is like drinking poison and hoping the other person would die."* You might think that by not forgiving someone, you are punishing him/her, but in fact, you are the one (sometimes, the only one) suffering. I have seen in many cases where people wouldn't forgive their spouses for things from as bad as cheating or abuse, to very trivial things

> If your intention is to have more joy and inner peace, then you have to learn to forgive and let go of your need to be right all the time.

that their spouses don't even remember. The sad thing is, sometimes their spouses didn't even know why they were mad in the first place. So, who is being punished?

Dr. Wayne Dyer has an analogy that I love. He said that the incident that caused you emotional pain is like a snakebite, and the resentment you have is like the snake venom. It's the venom, not the bite itself that will kill you. I have seen people who ruined wonderful relationships and their own happiness because they had to be right. They would rather die than forgive their loved ones, or admit they were wrong. It's truly tragic.

If your intention is to have more joy and inner peace, then you have to learn to forgive and let go of your need to be right all the time. As an African Proverb goes, *"Write the wrongs that are done to you in sand, but write the good things that happen to you on a piece of marble. Let go of all emotions such as resentment and retaliation, which diminish you, and hold onto the emotions such as gratitude and joy, which increase you."*

The Constant Mind Chatter

Besides resentment, many people also hold onto their childhood programming, which manifests as limiting beliefs, negative self-talk and self-sabotaging behaviors. These torment them emotionally, and hold them back from going after the career, relationship, or other goals they desire to achieve in life.

For example, many people believe that they are not good enough, smart enough, pretty enough, or they do not deserve it (be it love, money, success or happiness, for example). When you feel like you are not good enough and don't deserve it, you might procrastinate, hold yourself back, feel extremely anxious about failing and being rejected, try to please everyone around you at the cost of your own well-being, or feel guilty whenever you take time for yourself. You might feel like a fraud even when you are highly successful, and whatever you have achieved is never good enough.

It's very common. I bet you know someone who fits the above descriptions. Maybe you even identify with these feelings and behaviors yourself. In fact, everyone I've met has one of these limiting beliefs, in some shape or form, at least at one point of their lives. An extremely successful, Ivy-League-educated executive coach once confided in me that she used to have this limiting belief that she is not smart enough. I was speechless. She is one of the most intelligent people I know. It just goes to show you that it could happen to anyone. Some people are only mildly affected, others are completely paralyzed by their own

> **When you try to live up to unrealistic expectations, it's like attempting to achieve Mission Impossible, and you are destined to crash and burn (burnout). Then you beat yourself up even more for falling short, and become more convinced that there's something wrong with you. Your self-esteem plummets to a new low. The vicious cycle continues.**

limiting beliefs and undeserving mentality. Some people have overcome it, but, sadly, most are not even aware of their own limiting beliefs and programming. They keep trying and trying, not knowing that the root cause of their stress and the reason why they are not succeeding is their low self-esteem, undeserving mentality and self-defeating behaviors.

In coaching, I help my clients recognize and overcome these limiting beliefs and self-sabotaging behaviors so that they can have more inner peace and success in every area of their lives. I've always said that self-awareness is the first step toward change. As a coach, I serve as a mirror, or a flashlight to help my clients see the truth, so we can get to the root cause and solve the problem for good.

Miss Perfect
Many women I work with strive to be "perfect" all their lives, and beat themselves up for not living up to it. They often have very unrealistic expectations about what being perfect is, either based on their own beliefs or someone else's.

Think about the Super Mommy or Super Woman who thinks she should be able to excel at work, keep a spotless house, do homework with her children, cook a healthy dinner every night, chair the PTA committee, help her husband with his business, her children must get straight A's at school, everyone needs to look picture-perfect, and so on and so forth. Not only does she push herself to be perfect at all times, chances are she pushes *everyone* around her to meet her standards, too. She might be overly critical of other people, or thinks she is the only one who can do it right. For this reason, she is less likely to delegate or ask for help and more likely to complain that she is the only one who is doing all the work. If her children or someone she is caring for (patients, students, clients) are not making the kind of progress she would like, she is more likely to take it personally and perceive it as her own failure. She is also more likely to impose the same unrealistically high standards on her loved ones, and create much tension in her relationships. In her eyes, no one but she can do it right according to her standards. If she also buys into the irrational belief that asking for help is a sign of weakness and inadequacy, a perfectionist very often feels like she has to do it all, and ends up feeling exhausted and resentful.

Does this sound familiar? Maybe you know someone like that, or maybe you are one. Just imagine the pressure you are putting on yourself and your loved ones! When you try to live up to unrealistic expectations, it's like attempting to achieve Mission Impossible, and you are destined to crash and burn (burnout). Then you beat yourself up even more for falling short, and become more convinced that there's something wrong with you. Your self-esteem plummets to a new low. The vicious cycle continues.

Perfectionists often have a lot of self-imposed limitations. They try to play safe and draw inside the lines, because they are so afraid of making mistakes. In order to be "perfect", they might hold themselves back from expressing themselves authentically, or going after what they truly want, for fear of failure, rejection or being judged. It's like living in a self-imposed prison. As you can imagine, this creates much anxiety and stress in job performance, relationships, creativity, even how they dress themselves.

> "Perfection is an elusive butterfly. When we cease to demand perfection, the business of being happy becomes that much easier."
> -- Helen Keller

Another telltale symptom is procrastination. Perfectionists are so afraid of making mistakes that they often procrastinate. Their biggest fear is, "What if I put in 100% effort and the result is still not good enough?" That would prove once again that there is something wrong with them, and that would be too painful. So, instead, they procrastinate until the last minute to work on their projects. They can still finish the projects, but it might not be their best work. Or, they might not make it in time at all. At this point, they can then rationalize that it's because they did not have enough time, or did not try their best. It has nothing to do with their lack of ability.

Perfectionists feel compelled to strive for that perfection, according to their own standards, or the *perceived* expectations set by others. **At the core of perfectionism, I think, is the belief that "I am not good enough."**

If you are curious as to why I seem to know all this so well, it's because I am speaking as a recovering perfectionist. Yes, you heard me right. I have suffered the emotional turmoil and been stumped by many of the above challenges and setbacks due to perfectionism.

One of the many gifts of coaching, for me is the heightened self-awareness, tools and strategies I can use to help myself overcome such internal roadblocks to success and happiness. When a certain event triggers my perfectionism, instead of reacting to it by default and continuing the vicious cycle, I can catch myself and know that I can *choose* to respond differently. I wouldn't say that I am completely "cured" of perfectionism.

In fact, writing this book brought back so much insecurity in me, it's totally ridiculous. On one hand, I am so excited about making a small contribution to the world through this book and realizing my childhood dream as a published author. On the other hand, the thought of sharing my thoughts in print with the entire world is petrifying. The

> **Would you rather be perfect, or be happy? Would you choose to be right, or be at peace? If your goal is more joy, peace and time for yourself, choose wisely.**

perfectionism monster rears its ugly head, trying to force me to go back and hide in the cave with it. I have to really put my foot down and make a conscious choice to not let my perfectionism stop me in my tracks. The fact that you are reading this is a testament of my personal victory.

The Chipped China

When my husband and I got married, we made a deal. I will gladly cook if he does the dishes. It's been over 15 years, and I'm proud to say that we have both kept our end of the bargain. Of course, if you look closely at the dishes and utensils in our house, you will see that they are not always spotless. In fact, many of them are chipped on the edge, or sometimes have some food stuck on them. I used to cringe when I saw chipped china or a dirty spoon.

Now I just chuckle and put the dirty spoon in the sink. The kids think it's funny or yucky, depending on their moods. Obviously, washing the dishes is not one of the strong suits of my brilliant Ph.D. husband. In fact, he has

> Graciously accept any assistance others offer you, and ask for help when you can really use it. It's not a sign of inadequacy; it's an act of self-love.

a tendency of breaking stuff, like the time he broke one of the soup bowls of our brand new dinner set as soon as we got home from the store. What can I say? If I have to choose between a perfect china set and a happy marriage, I'd always choose the latter.

Would you rather be perfect, or be happy? Would you choose to be right, or be at peace? If your goal is more joy, peace and time for yourself, choose wisely. I often joke with my clients that the last time I checked, the Academy Awards does not have a category called Best Martyr of the Year. So why are you working so hard to win the award that does not exist?

Graciously accept any assistance others offer you, and ask for help when you can really use it. It's not a sign of inadequacy; it's an act of self-love. The dishes might not be done the way you want them, but you will have more time to relax or do something you love.

My new rule about clutter, whether material or emotional, is to get rid of anything that isn't useful, beautiful or joyful. Try it on and see how much lighter you will feel.

Self-Coaching Session
De-Clutter for Inner Peace

✳ What are the thoughts and beliefs that are causing you stress and anxiety?

✳ When you have these thoughts and beliefs, how are you feeling physically?

✳ How are you feeling emotionally when these thoughts and beliefs enter your mind?

✳ What's your action (or lack of action) as a result of such feelings?

* What are the results you experience, and how are they affecting your life right now (for example, your level of stress, health, productivity, relationship, self-esteem, level of success)?

* If you continue to hold on to these thoughts and beliefs, how will they affect your life in the long run?

* What are you willing to let go, in order to have less stress, more joy and inner peace?

* What's the first step you are committed to take today?

Key #3

Fast Track to Calm

It is important from time to time to slow down, to go away by yourself, and simply be.
-- Eileen Caddy, Scottish writer and spiritual leader

Where's the Brake?

Does your life look like a race car running at break-neck speed and, to your horror, the brakes are broken? Do you feel like you are perpetually in a hurry, even when you are not in a hurry to go anywhere? Do you feel like all the items on your to-do list are dancing around in your head, and you can't seem to concentrate on any of them? Do you run around like a chicken without a head all day, and still feel like you will never catch up? Has it occurred to you that you have forgotten how to relax? You are not alone.

Many of my coaching clients come to me, all frazzled and stressed, brimming with anxiety that they will never get it all done, or get it done the "right" way. They want to learn how to manage their stress, and create some balance in their lives, but they simply do not know how to relax. You'd be surprised how many people draw a complete blank when I ask them what they do for fun, or what relaxes them. It's so sad that they have become so disconnected from themselves. Annie is one such example. She told me that even when she was at the spa, she could not totally relax because half way through her massage she was already thinking about what she had to get done after the spa.

Addicted to Speed

With so much to do, and so little time, how do you deal? Many people tell me they try to become more efficient so they can *squeeze* more tasks in a day. Some proudly tell me that they thrive on stress under deadlines. Can you relate to this?

> **When you feel overwhelmed and your life is spinning out of control, instead of trying to work faster and harder, you should try to deliberately S-L-O-W D-O-W-N.**

What you may not realize is that you have been running on adrenaline. When we are under stress (whether physical or emotional), it triggers the fight-or-flight response in our body, which is then flushed with adrenaline to help us deal with the crisis at hand. Adrenaline is like caffeine that pumps us up with extra energy and alertness. It's referred to as an adrenaline rush because it's highly addictive. You feel so much more productive and on top of everything. However, just like how caffeine affects your body, once the adrenaline rush is over, you experience a "crash."

Some people try to stay in that adrenaline rush so they won't experience the crash. The problem is, when you are stressed, your body is flooded with extra amount of adrenaline as well as cortisol. Research has repeatedly linked these powerful stress hormones to increased risks of heart disease, hypertension, stroke, obesity, sleep disorder, etc. In other words, unchecked chronic stress can wreck havoc on your health.

There is a Chinese saying that's similar to "*Haste makes waste*." **The fastest way is not necessarily the best way to get you where you want to go. Sometimes, when you try to rush somewhere, you end up not arriving at all.**

Fast Track to Calm
When people ask me how to reduce stress quickly, I tell them to take a deep breath and slow down. I know this

might sound counter-intuitive, and I have mentioned this concept in a previous chapter, *Stop, Drop and Roll Out of Overwhelm*, but it's worth repeating. When you feel overwhelmed and your life is spinning out of control, instead of trying to work faster and harder, you should try to deliberately S-L-O-W D-O-W-N. Ideally, you want to create some white space in your life, that is, pockets of quiet time to rest, meditate, reflect, stop and smell the roses. You want to live in the present moment, and truly be where you are. Just like Chinese paintings need adequate white space to maintain the balance, so does your life.

Tao of the Unhurried Life

Here are some ideas to help you slow down and practice what I call *Tao of the Unhurried Life.*

1. Watch Your Breathing

Research shows that when you focus all of your attention on one thing, your heart rate slows down and blood pressure lowers. The easiest way to achieve this is to observe your breathing. We tend to hold our breath or breathe too shallow when we are stressed. When you find yourself tense or holding your breath, take a few deep breaths. Then breathe normally for a minute or two, while focusing your attention entirely on breathing in and out. Your mind will interrupt you with all kinds of ideas and thoughts. That's normal. When you notice a thought, just observe it, without judging it, and let it go. Return to observing your breathing.

This is a basic relaxation technique and the beginner level of meditation. Sounds simple, but it's not easy to do. We are so used to running and doing stuff all the time that most people have forgotten why we are called human

> Create some white space in your life, that is, pockets of quiet time to rest, meditate, reflect, stop and smell the roses. You want to live in the present moment, and truly be where you are. Just like Chinese paintings need adequate white space to maintain the balance, so does your life.

"being," not human "doing." If you have difficulty focusing at the beginning, don't worry. Start with 1-3 minutes, and work up to 30 minutes if you can.

2. Stop Speed-Eating

Even if you are not interested in practicing mindfulness, you should really slow down when you eat. Eating on the run produces anxiety and stress, which interferes with digestion. Studies show that when people eat quickly, they tend to overeat. That's because when you eat fast, your brain does not have enough time to register that you are already full, and that you should stop eating. As a result of stress (remember that stress hormone cortisol contributes to weight gain) and overeating, you end up gaining weight.

A recent WebMD article lists speed-eating as the No. 1 diet mistake (skipping meals is No. 2 on the list). Another study showed that when you sit down to eat a snack instead of eating on the run, you are less tempted to eat other snacks later on. It seems like when we are "eating on the go," our brain often doesn't register how full we are, which is another reason to practice mindful eating, instead of speed eating.

So, try to sit down and savor your food. If you don't have time to sit down and relax at every meal, at least make a conscious effort to eat one meal in peace every day. Unplug the phone, TV, computer and your Blackberry. Be fully present and eat in peace.

3. Allow Enough Time

In our over-scheduled, always-rushing life style, we often under-estimate how much time each task takes, or over-estimate how much we can get done in the amount of time we have. As a result, we are always running late and stressed. When you schedule your appointments, try to allow 1.5 times of your original estimated time. Also, allow enough travel time between appointments. That way, if you hit traffic, you won't go crazy. I always keep good books, CDs, my iPod with a teleclass I want to listen to, water, and snacks in my purse and my car. I pick out a book that I'm dying to read when I need to go to doctor's office. That way, when I'm stuck in traffic or at the doctor's office, I don't feel like I'm losing time. On the contrary, I'm gaining valuable time by reading the books that I might otherwise have no time to read.

4. Create Smooth Transitions

How about the transition between work and home? How often do you rush home and, without taking a break, jump right in to your "other job" at home? It's important to allow yourself enough time and space to make that transition. When you are coming home from work, create some kind of ritual to signal the end of your work day, and prepare yourself for the transition back to home life. Take an extra 10-15 minutes to walk in the park, stop by your favorite coffee shop or a book store, before going home. You can also sit in your car and listen to some soothing music, meditate or read something funny. A client of mine would drive around the block or sit in the car on his own driveway for a few minutes, until he was ready to re-join the rest of the family.

On my front door I have taped a picture of a smiling cat with two Chinese sentences I copied from a story I once read. In the story, there was a couple who would come home from work stressed and irritated, leading to fights between them. The wife then decided to put a wooden sign on their front door that reads, "*Upon entering this door, please take off your troubles. When you come home, bring happiness with you.*" It's a great reminder for me and my husband to leave work at work and not let the stress of the day enter into our family life.

Try to create a smooth transition between work and home. Find a routine that helps you brighten your mood before you re-join your family for the evening. Believe me, you will feel much calmer when you walk in the door.

5. Clear the Way for Calm

In order to slow down and have enough time, you need to de-clutter your home and your schedule. An organized home gives you a sense of serenity and provides a safe haven for you to relax and recharge. On the other hand, to cut down on the tasks in your schedule, you need to say no and set good boundaries.

Take an honest look at your commitments. How many do you really enjoy? How many can be done by someone else? Do you take on additional commitments because you want to, or because you think you should? Or, perhaps you take them on just because you don't know how to say no? Protect your time like it's the most valuable asset you have. Since we all have 24 hours a day, when you say yes to something, you are saying no to something else. So choose carefully. What would you rather be doing?

Above all, you need to realize that you cannot do everything and be everything for everyone. It's okay to let go of some of the tasks so that you have time and energy to take care of what truly matters to you (that includes taking good care of yourself). It's okay to say no and ask for help when you need it! Asking for support is not a sign of inadequacy or incompetence. Rather, it's an act of self- love. You don't have to go it alone. Really.

When you can honor your own needs and priorities, ask for support when you need it, take proactive steps to eliminate stress and nurture yourself on a regular basis, you will be able to avoid burnout, safeguard your well-being and, in the long run, the well-being of your loved ones. And you'll be on the fast track to true peace and calm.

Self-Coaching Session
Fast Track to Calm

∗ In what area(s) of your life do you feel rushed, overwhelmed, or out of control? Why?

∗ What would you like to experience instead? Write down the specific conditions, attitude, or behaviors that would make your life less stressful, more enjoyable, or create more time for you.

✳ What could get in the way? Write down the conditions, thoughts and beliefs that could interfere with your intention to slow down and take more time for you.

✳ In what way can you slow down? Out of the ideas shared in this chapter, which one(s) would you like to try out in your life?

∗ What new ritual or routine can you practice daily, to create more mindfulness and calm in your life?

∗ Take out your calendar, and schedule some White Space (or Me Time) for the next couple weeks.

Key #4

Opt-In for Joy

Life in itself is an empty canvas; it becomes whatsoever you paint on it. You can paint misery, you can paint bliss. This freedom is your glory.

-- Osho, Indian Spiritual Teacher

Cheryl's Story

Years ago, I coached Cheryl who was not very happy with her current career. She said that it was a very nice, secure and good-paying job, and everyone around her told her she should be happy with it. However, she just didn't feel any passion or fulfillment any longer. Then she said to me, "Sometimes, I wish I could be hit by a bus so I don't have to go to work." I had to stop her right there, "Did you hear what you just said?" It's such a shocking and revealing statement of her state of mind. I then helped her work on getting clarity about her ideal career, and carve out action steps to make the change.

Joy-Starved

Somehow, her statement stayed with me. I think of it from time to time, whenever I meet someone who is not happy with his/her career. Last month, I gave a workshop on the secrets of successful midlife career change. The room was packed and they even had to turn away many participants. Obviously there are a lot of professionals in transition or contemplating a midlife career change. As I talked to them, I found out that although some of them entered career transitions involuntarily, many are proactively seeking a new career for higher personal fulfillment. That's where life coaching or career coaching can be extremely valuable, to help you get clarity in what you truly desire in a career, and map out an action plan to obtain such a career. Anyway, during the workshop, when I shared my client's story and her moment-of-truth statement, one gentleman in the back stood up and said that he had the same thought before, and he knew others who had probably thought of the same

> **Joy is your true nature and birthright. Life is meant to be joyful. Suffering is so over-rated.**

thing even though they would not admit it. How interesting, I thought, considering how strong my client's statement was. Then several other participants echoed his sentiment and shared their own experiences of feeling unfulfilled, or even flat-out miserable at work. Obviously the number of people unhappy with their career is significant. I just didn't expect so many people felt such strong feelings about their current careers. How miserable do you have to be at work that you'd prefer to be hit by a bus or truck?!!

Your Joy Quotient

Aristotle said, *"Pleasure in the job puts perfection in the work."* It really saddens me to see people stay in a career in which they feel no joy, or are downright miserable. From my years of coaching and counseling experiences, I know most people are low on Joy Quotient in their lives. Think about it. If you are like most people, you spend most of your waking hours at work (either paid or not). So, if you feel unhappy at work, it can easily affect your personal life and lower your overall Joy Quotient.

And it's not just at work that people might be joy-challenged. When I give a workshop on life balance, I usually have participants do a Wheel of Balance exercise. In this exercise, you give a score on each of eight different areas of your life to reflect how satisfied you are in that area. These eight areas are: Personal Growth, Self-Care, Family, Career, Finance, Relationship, Community and Fun (in no particular order of importance). **Over the years, what I've found, consistently, is that the majority of people score really low on the area of fun.** In fact, most people give themselves a score below four, on a scale of one to ten, ten being most satisfied in that area. When I ask my workshop participants (mostly women) what they do for fun, there are always people who stare at me as if I am speaking a foreign language. Some would ask: "Fun? What do you mean fun? Who has time for that?!!" When I probe, some would say, "Oh I used to do such and such, but that was years ago, before my kids were born (or before I changed career, or before my mom got sick, etc.)" Can you relate to this?

Such response is also consistent with my private coaching clients. Many are professional women or business owners in caregiving roles either in their personal or professional lives. One of my clients Carol came to the realization that she was all consumed by caring for her mom that she no longer had time for self-care or fun in her life, and she felt stressed and resentful. Another client

> "Reduce your workload by 30% and increase your fun load by 30% and you will increase your revenues by 100%. And you will increase your productivity by 10,000% (If there could be such percentage.). More fun, less struggle -- more results on all fronts." -- Abraham-Hicks

Angie told me that she was so busy building her business that there was no room for fun in her life any more. She told me that she used to read many books for leisure, work out, and go out with her girlfriends. Since she started her own business, everything she reads and listens to is all business related. **When I probe deeper, I helped my clients see that one of the reasons they are fun-starved is that they no longer give themselves permission to have fun, until all their work is done.** Since they can never complete everything on their mile-long to-do list, they decide, either consciously or subconsciously, that they simply cannot afford to have fun.

Joy is Your True Nature

I beg to differ. In fact, I'd like to argue that you simply cannot afford not to have joy and fun in your life. You may think that completing your to-do list for home and work will make life better. Then why is it that the harder you work, the harder you work? Do you believe that life is all about work, work, work, and nothing but work? Some people actually told me life is about suffering. How sad is that?

It's not your fault if you do feel this way. Just like my clients, most of us were told by our parents and/or teachers that, "You must finish all the work before you can play." They meant to help us cultivate a strong work ethic.

If you are a parent, you have probably told your child the same thing. My dad is a strong believer that you must work hard all the time, while my belief is "work hard, play hard", which of course did not sit well with him. I remember having many conversations with my dad on this issue, ever since I was in preschool or kindergarten. Even as a young child, I instinctively knew that it's good to have a balance between work and play. I think most of us had the same instinct when we were very young, and somewhere on our journey we bought into the belief that we must not play unless all work is done.

Of course, there is nothing wrong with a strong work ethic. **The problem is, when is our work ever "done"? As seasoned grownups, we all know too well that our work is never done. Does it mean we should never have fun?** I hope your reaction is, "Don't be ridiculous, of course we should still have fun!"

Rumi wrote, *"The soul is here for its own joy."* Joy is your true nature and birthright. Life is meant to be joyful. Suffering is so over-rated.

Rx for Joy

So what can you do to have more joy and fun in your life? Here are some ideas for you.

1. Give Yourself Permission

In order to experience more joy in your life, you need to first have the intention and give yourself permission to have joy. So many people have the hang ups about being in joy. For example, they might feel guilty, selfish, undeserving, or think it's unrealistic to have joy. They don't think they have enough time or money or energy. They say they want more joy, but they don't really give themselves permission to have it. Or they believe that their joy depends on other people, things, or life circumstances. Since

> In order to experience more joy in your life, you need to first have the intention and give yourself permission to have joy.

joy is out of their control, they feel like a victim. How about you? What's your story? Whatever your story is, it separates you from your joy. You need to make a conscious choice to let it go.

2. Find Your Innate Joy

The truth is, joy is your true nature and your birthright. You are born with innate joy. It's already in you. It does not reside outside of you. It does not depend on other people or any material things. It doesn't even depend on your life circumstances. Have you ever met people who have endured horrific circumstances and still are brimming with joy? You do not need to search or strive for joy. It doesn't always cost money to have joy, either. Sometimes the greatest joy is the simplest. All children innately know how to be in joy, but most grown-ups have forgotten how. You simply need to re-learn how to tap into it. And the first step is to realize and embrace that joy is already within you, and you need to give yourself permission to experience joy.

3. Put Your Attention on Joy

More likely than not, your attention is on lack of joy, instead of the joy you have in your life. According to the Law of Attraction, whatever you focus your attention on, expands. If you focus on what you don't have and what's not working, you are more likely to see more of what's wrong in your life, and you won't experience joy. On the other hand, if you choose to focus on joy, you are more likely to notice and experience more joy. I'm sure you have experienced joy in the past. What does joy feel like to you? What kinds of sensations do you feel in

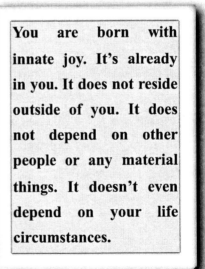

You are born with innate joy. It's already in you. It does not reside outside of you. It does not depend on other people or any material things. It doesn't even depend on your life circumstances.

your body, your heart and your mind? What brings you joy? What would you like to experience more? What can do you to create such opportunities? **Really pay attention to your joy. Study it. Observe it. Be it.**

4. Seize the Moment

Sometimes joy and fun come at "inconvenient" times. How many times have you turned down a spontaneous opportunity to have more joy and fun because your work is not done, or there are dirty dishes in the sink, or your hair is not perfect? How many times have you turned down an impromptu dinner invitation because you have already thawed something? How many times has your child excitedly asked you to look at something, or play with her, and you let her wait until it's too late?

I once read an article written by a woman who tried to ask her sister out for lunch numerous times. Each time her sister had different reasons why she couldn't have lunch, for example, there's something on the stove or in the washer, it looks like rain, she is having a bad hair day or a headache, and the list goes on and on. It was written in a light-hearted tone, and I was chuckling over all the excuses her sister gave her until I read the last paragraph. Her sister passed away suddenly, and they never had lunch.

Life is too short to miss out on joy and precious moments you can share with your loved ones. Nobody is guaranteed tomorrow. You never know when would be your last day or last time with someone you care about might be. Instead of complaining about your caregiving responsibilities or being interrupted from work, why not appreciate the opportunity to spend time with your loved one and create memory you can both treasure? Next time, when your child eagerly pulls you to play with her, your mom calls just to chat, or your friend invites you to a girls' night out, if it will bring you joy, just say yes. If you have been thinking about picking up an old hobby or learning how to dance, or visiting a girlfriend you haven't seen for months, make it happen. The housework can wait, but the opportunity to experience pure joy may never return if you miss it.

5. Go Out of Your Comfort Zone

Have you ever experienced the euphoria of succeeding at something way out of your comfort zone? The adrenaline rush and the "If I can do this, I can do *anything*" feeling is exhilarating! **Unlike the short-lived happiness of buying something new, the joy of achieving something out of your comfort zone stays with you forever.** I'm fortunate to have many such experiences in my life: when I moved to a foreign country to study for my master's degree, received my black belt in Tae Kwon Do, competed and won my first state championship gold medal, tried ocean kayaking, learned to fence and gave my first keynote speech, just to name a few. My friend Christina told me that she went to a seminar where she did a fire walk and broke a board. Surprisingly, the experience gave her a great sense of serenity. It somehow helped her cope with caring for her mom who was having a lot of health problems at the time.

Of course, you don't have to try something so dramatic as walking through fire, training for a black belt, or skydiving. It can be something like learning a new language, trying a new recipe, running a 5K race, or traveling somewhere alone. The point is to try something you have never done before.

> **When you stretch yourself, you will have increased self-confidence and the joy of achieving something new. When you have more confidence, you will naturally feel calmer, knowing you can handle anything that comes your way.**

When you stretch yourself, you will have increased self-confidence and the joy of achieving something new. When you have more confidence, you will naturally feel calmer, knowing you can handle anything that comes your way. Right now, you might be facing some challenges in your life that require you to stretch yourself and get out of your comfort zone. Instead of retreating or complaining, take it on.

The Shortcut to Joy

There is a fail-proof way to experience joy quickly, and that is to count your blessings. No matter what your current circumstances are, when you can focus your attention on what you are grateful for, you will instantaneously be connected and infused with your innate joy. One of the exercises I often give my coaching clients is to go through their day actively looking for the Top Three Things that happen to them that day. Whenever a better thing happens, they will replace one of the items on their Top Three Things list. Alternatively, you can keep adding the good things to your list until the end of the day. You can do this exercise by keeping a mental list or by writing down your list on a piece of paper you carry throughout the day. At the end of the day, you can review the list, take a moment to express

> No matter what your current circumstances are, when you can focus your attention on what you are grateful for, you will instantaneously be connected and infused with your innate joy.

your gratitude for these good things, and write them in your journal if you like.

You will find that on some days you have great things that happen to you, and other days, it's hard to find anything good. That's normal. We all have ups and downs. Even on a difficult day, if you pay attention, you can find something to be grateful for, even if it's something as small as a smile from a complete stranger. Just keep focusing on the good things, big and small, and you will be filled with joy every day.

Life is supposed to be enjoyed, not endured. Ralph Waldon Emerson said, *"Allow yourself to trust joy and embrace it. You will find you dance with everything."* What can you do to bring more joy into your everyday life? **Whatever feeds your soul and makes your heart sing, go with it.**

Self-Coaching Session
Opt-In for Joy

✳ What brings you joy? Finish this sentence: "I feel joy when...."

✳ What do you feel in your body, your heart and your mind when you experience joy?

✷ What joyful experiences would you like to have in your life?

✷ How can you create such experiences? Write down a few ideas and action steps. Ask someone to brainstorm with you if you can't think of anything.

* What help can you enlist to create more joy and fun in your life?

* Take out your calendar, and schedule some fun time for the next couple weeks.

Key #5

In-the-Moment Serenity

Do not dwell in the past, do not dream of the future,
concentrate the mind on the present moment.
-- Buddha

Past, Present, Future

Most people either live in the past with regrets or resentment, or in the future with endless worries and what ifs. When you think about it, you can only be present now, not yesterday or tomorrow. Unless you have a time machine, there is nothing you can do to change events in the past. As for the future, spending time and energy in worries and fears really doesn't help at all.

From an evolutionary standpoint, it's human nature to review our past experiences and constantly evaluate our situation so we can learn from our past and avoid danger in the future. It's an important survival skill. The problem is, when you overdo it, you become filled with stress and negative emotions that paralyze you and prevent you from living life to the fullest. While you are engrossed in reliving the past or worrying about the future, you are missing what's going on, right here and right now, in your life.

What's worse, since part of your time and energy is consumed by these negative emotions, you are left with less energy to handle what is going on right now. You are more likely to have a hard time focusing, make more mistakes, or become paralyzed by stress and fears that you cannot function at your optimal level. This will cause a huge problem when you are required to make important decisions, or perform physically and emotionally taxing tasks such as caregiving.

> While you are engrossed in reliving the past, or worrying about the future, you are missing what's going on, right here and right now, in your life.

The Point of Power

Our lives are made up by all the moments we experience. However, we can only experience one moment at a time. All we have, and all we can affect, is the present moment. It's not hard then to understand that the point of power is in the present moment... right here and right now.

In this world where everything seems to come at you at break-neck speed, focusing on the present moment becomes especially challenging. Thoughts and emotions about the past and future are competing with endlessly multiplying to-do's on any given day. You are playing multiple roles at home and at work, with a multitude of responsibilities. You already feel like you are juggling too many things and being pulled from every direction. On top of that, the mass media is broadcasting 24/7 all the bad news from every corner of the world, the phone is ringing off the hook, and you are constantly bombarded by emails, text messages and instant messages. Is it any wonder that you are so stressed?

> Our lives are made up by all the moments we experience. However, we can only experience one moment at a time. All we have, and all we can affect, is the present moment. It's not hard then to understand that the point of power is in the present moment... right here and right now.

The Multitasking Trap

There's so much to do, and never enough time. In order to cope, most people try to multitask as much as they can, hoping it will save them time and get more accomplished. However, study after study has shown that multitasking doesn't always help, especially when it comes to tasks that require logical thinking and concentration. Our brains are wired to process one thing at a time. When you try to perform two tasks that require logical thinking, your brain has to constantly start and re-start in order to switch between the tasks. It actually slows down your process time. In fact, many studies showed that multitasking decreases productivity and increases human errors, not to mention the stress and anxiety that come with it.

Just imagine, your thoughts are constantly jumping among past regrets, future worries, and all the tasks and external stimuli in the present. How can you not feel stressed and overwhelmed?

Lessons from the Fencing Strip

Last Spring, I decided to try saber fencing with my then 10-year-old son. My only prior experience with any sword is Tai Chi Sword. While there are a few similar moves, it is of course very different from fencing. As you know, fencing is quite a high-skilled sport. Learning something this challenging is very exciting.

At the beginning, we spent all our class time practicing basic drills over and over. They were simple and repetitive. It made me wonder how I was going to handle a real fencing match. Gradually, we learned some new drills and started very short fencing matches at the end of the class. At first, I was very nervous. Intellectually, I knew there was no real danger in fencing. We are well-protected by our gear and it's much safer than martial arts sparring. Nonetheless, I was still nervous. My body was all tight, I had a death grip on my saber, and I was over-thinking which maneuver I should use. It was physically and mentally exhausting. After a while, I gradually loosened up. I finally stopped over-thinking and let my instincts take over. Because I was calmer and fully present, I could see my opponent's moves more clearly, too. It's as if I was "in the zone". My head was clear and time disappeared. Nothing else in the world existed. To my surprise, in those times I was able to use the correct maneuvers out of reflex. And, I wasn't stressed or tired after the match.

This really taught me something. I remember going through the same process with Tae Kwon Do and Tai Chi Sword training. It was after I could manage to relax and be fully in the moment, that my skills progressed and I was able to enjoy the art.

In addition, I found these trainings to be a great antidote to the stress in my life. Whatever stress I was experiencing at work or at home does not exist when I was in class. I was able to forget everything for the moment, and just enjoy doing something I love. After all, when there's a sword or a fist coming at you, it's really hard to think about the deadline or to-do list. It's as therapeutic as practicing yoga or meditation.

In-the-Moment Serenity

Have you ever had experiences where you are "in the zone" and everything else disappears except for what you are doing? Time does not exist because you are totally focused in the moment. The constant chatter in your head about the past, the future, your insecurity, all the fears and what ifs disappear, too. You are left with complete peace and quiet. There is only you and that one single thing you are doing. Someone once said, there are no stressful events, only stressful thoughts. Since most of your stress comes from your stressful thoughts, when you can silence your mind and be completely in the moment, there is no

> Someone once said, there are no stressful events, only stressful thoughts. Since most of your stress comes from your stressful thoughts, when you can silence your mind and be completely in the moment, there is no stress.

stress. It doesn't matter if you are doing something fun or performing brain surgery. Even if you are dealing with a crisis situation, when you are fully present without being bombarded by the worries, fears and all the other things going on in your life, you can think more clearly and better solve the problems at hand. You'll be able to see the big picture, and focus on handling one task at a time without the unnecessary stress from your mind.

Here are a few tips to help you live in the present moment and create moment to moment serenity.

1. Practice Mindfulness

Years ago, a friend introduced me to Jon Kabat-Zinn and Thich Nhat Hanh's books on mindfulness meditation. I quickly fell in love with their work. Mindfulness is considered the heart of Buddhist meditation. According to Jon Kabat-Zinn, the director of the Stress Reduction Clinic at the University of Massachusetts Medical Center, **mindfulness is moment-to-moment, non-judgmental awareness**. It's a tool to bridge the gap between doing and being, and bring us back to the here-and-now.

Our mind is often on auto-pilot, and we are not fully "awake" in the present moment. You might be physically here, but your mind is completely somewhere else. Without mindfulness, you are not fully present in your own lives, and in your relationships with others.

Jon Kabat-Zinn has been using mindfulness practice and techniques in his clinic to successfully help the patients manage stress, panic, fears, anxiety, physical pain, emotional pain, sleep problems, and promote healing from all types of illnesses. To demonstrate mindfulness, he asked his stress-reduction program participants how they eat raisins. Most people eat them by the handful. I'm sure you do too. However, he asked the participants to eat one single raisin, engage all five senses, and really experience its full flavor and texture. I tried that, and it opened my eyes. Now when I need a reminder of mindfulness, I take a raisin, or a very small piece of dark chocolate, and eat it as slowly as I can.

You can practice mindfulness meditation anytime, anywhere, in everything you do. I once studied with a very high-level master in a rare Chinese internal martial art. He taught me the basic standing meditation that's the

> **Mindfulness is moment-to-moment, non-judgmental awareness. It is a tool to bridge the gap between doing and being, and bring us back to the here-and-now. If you focus 100% of your attention on whatever you are doing. Then, everything you do will be a mindfulness meditation.**

foundational training of that internal art. One day I asked him what to do when I didn't have time to practice the standing meditation, and he said, "Then do every task in the same manner as you do meditation." It's the same principle as the mindfulness practice. Whether you are working, eating, reading, washing dishes, walking the dog, or pumping iron at the gym, try focusing 100% of your attention on whatever you are doing. Then, everything you do will be a mindfulness meditation.

2. Avoid Multitasking

Needless to say, if your goal is relaxation and inner peace, multi-tasking is not the way to go. As I wrote in an earlier chapter, multitasking often creates more anxiety and stress without producing better results. My coach told me she used to listen to her voice mail while reading her emails. The result was a lot of mistakes and anxiety. I can't tell you how many times I made a wrong turn, because I was driving and trying to carry on a conversation. Let me give you another example. Have you ever opened too many programs and windows on your computer? Does this slow down your computer, or speed up the process? If you have ever experienced a computer freeze up, you know what I'm talking about.

3. Minimize Distractions

It's really hard to be fully present when you have distractions all around you. In our 24/7 multi-media world, it's quite easy to become over-stimulated and distracted. I suspect that many people feel like they have ADD/ADHD, at least once in a while. If you don't watch it, you could easily follow the next "shiny object" and get totally lost in the bottomless rabbit hole. Before you know it, you have lost many valuable hours and your work is still not done. The stress and anxiety kick in, and you can't stop kicking yourself. Sound familiar?

Instead of allowing the distractions to sidetrack you and create unnecessary stress, take action to minimize distractions in your environment. Some people have the habit of leaving the TV news on in the background all day long, which is really a bad idea. In order to keep stress and anxiety in check, I believe that our mind and body need proper amounts of quiet time. Besides, most of the news on TV is really negative and would only make you more anxious and stressed. Why in the world would you choose to fill your mind with this kind of toxin?

When you need to focus on tasks, turn off your telephone, BlackBerry, TV, radio, email, AIM, Internet and/or computer (unless you need that for your task). Close the door if possible and let others know not to interrupt you.

Set a timer for 15 to 50 minutes, depending on your task, and commit to working with your undivided attention until the timer goes off. Do not work more than 50 minutes at a time without taking a break, though. Our attention span is limited. If you force yourself to work longer without proper rest, you will lose focus and productivity. Whether you are at work or at home, keep distractions and stimuli minimal. You will be able to focus on the present moment and feel more relaxed.

4. Take Time for You

Last but not least, take time for you. Most people don't realize they are over-extended and heading for burnout. The truth is, you might not realize it unless you can slow down enough to see your reality. Some of my clients come to this realization after carefully examining their schedules, core values and priorities during our coaching sessions. Some tell me that

> **Make a conscious choice to put self-care as a top priority. After all, if you don't nurture yourself, you won't have any more to give.**

everything they do is related to their responsibilities at work and at home, and they do not have the time to do things just for themselves. They have forgotten what they used to do just for fun.

If you can relate to this, it's time for some Intensive Self-Care! Make a conscious choice to put self-care as a top priority. After all, if you don't nurture yourself, you won't have any more to give.

Schedule "Me Time" on a daily, or at least weekly basis. Do something good for yourself every day. It could be something small, like buying yourself some fresh flowers, or spending half an hour reading, or taking a bubble bath. Or, it could be something big, like a spa day or girls' night out. **It's helpful to find at least one activity that you enjoy that can help you practice being fully present and temporarily forget the challenges in your life.** Do whatever pleases you. Savor every moment. Be fully present. Then you will experience in-the-moment serenity.

Self-Coaching Session
In-the-Moment Serenity

✳ Do you spend a lot of time thinking about past events or worrying about the future? If so, write them down here.

✳ Pay attention to your thoughts. Whenever your thoughts wander to the past or the future, in a negative way, pause and bring your attention back to the present moment.

∗ Find a few ways to help you focus on here and now. If deep breathing and meditation are not your thing, you can also try using a mantra such as "Here and Now" or "Breathe", whenever you feel a need to re-focus your attention in the present moment.

∗ What activity do you enjoy that can help you practice being fully present, and temporarily forget about the challenges in your life?

Key #6

Practice Detached Involvement

"Have a heart that is open to everything, and attached to nothing."
-- Dr. Wayne Dyer

Grandpa's Story

There are experiences in life that are significant to us. They teach us lessons never to be forgotten. When I was 13 years old, I had one such unforgettable experience.

My grandfather was a medical doctor who specialized in gastrointestinal diseases, including liver diseases and liver cancer. Ironically, he was diagnosed with liver cancer himself. The doctors told my parents that it was inoperable and grandpa had three to six months at most. He decided against chemotherapy and chose to stay home instead. My mom told me that one of her uncles was a doctor of Chinese medicine, and he gave Grandpa Chinese herbs for liver health and pain management.

Grandpa quit, cold turkey, a lifetime of smoking and drinking, and kept a very simple life. Incredibly, he lived for 21 months.

This occurred when I was in middle school. My grandparents lived with us. I remember visiting their suite every day after school. Grandpa was a man of few words, while Grandma was the life of the party. Of course, Grandpa was more active before he became ill. When I was 10, he practiced medicine in Japan. When my younger sister Phoebe and I visited them, Grandpa and Grandma took us to all the famous tourist spots in Tokyo and surrounding cities. That summer, Phoebe and I had an experience of a lifetime. However, in his last year of life, I remember Grandpa being much more subdued and quiet. Mom told me that they actually never told Grandpa his cancer diagnosis (it's a common practice in my culture), but, she believed that Grandpa must have known, being a doctor himself. Remarkably, I didn't see a streak of anger, fear or depression in Grandpa. I'm sure he went through the grieving process privately, and came to the acceptance stage. All I saw and felt was a sense of peace and calm around him. At least that's what I remember. Grandpa faced his death with such grace.

All the King's Horses

On the contrary, Dad was the one in anguish. I saw first hand the frustration, pain, guilt, regret, sense of powerlessness and defeat that my dad went through. There are ironies on multiple levels. Not only was my grandpa a medical doctor specializing in liver diseases, he had two sons and one son-in-law who were also medical doctors, and a daughter-in-law (my mom) who was a registered nurse. My dad and uncles had a great network of doctor friends and some of them were the top experts in the largest medical center in my country. All the king's horses and all the king's men couldn't save Grandpa from cancer!

This was my first encounter with cancer. It was such a humbling lesson about the limitations of medicine and how little we can do in the face of death. Less than two years later, Grandma passed too. She had just come back from a month of European vacation and fell ill. It was so sudden. She passed away in three months. Until this day, I still cannot believe that she is gone.

Finding Peace in the Face of Death

Partially because of Grandpa, when I became an RN, I chose the same specialty (gastroenterology) as Grandpa did and worked in the largest medical center in Taiwan. Besides a garden variety of digestive diseases, many of my patients had hepatitis and cancers of the liver, stomach, pancreas, and many of them were terminal patients. When you take care of a patient for a while and build a good relationship, it's heart-breaking to know that he/she is losing the battle and there's nothing you can do to change that outcome. Even with such personal experiences with cancer and caregiving, I still had a hard time in the beginning. For a while I used to go home physically and emotionally exhausted, and dreaded going to work the next day because some of my patients might have passed away while I was not there. I knew it was not my fault or anyone's fault, but I just couldn't help but feel depressed, powerless, and defeated.

> **I learned to practice** *detached involvement.* **I realized that all I could do was give them the best care I could and let go of trying to control the outcome, if I were to have any peace of mind.**

Then, gradually I came to acknowledge my own feelings, and accept that I simply could not control or change the fact that my patients were terminally ill. They were dying and it had nothing to with my nursing skills or who I was. Slowly, I learned to practice *detached involvement.* I realized that all I could do was give them the best care I could and let go of trying to control the outcome, if I were to have any peace of mind.

It took me a while to learn that lesson, and I'm so glad I did. **The ability to practice detached involvement has helped me tremendously in my roles as a nurse, counselor, life coach, business owner, and mother.**

Parenting Nightmare

A few years ago, when Prince Harry made front page news for making a scene at a party, I couldn't help but think how awful Princess Diana would have felt if she was still alive. She had sacrificed so much to give her sons a "normal" life, and I'm sure she had made her best efforts to raise them to be honorable, respectable, outstanding human beings. She probably would have felt disappointed and broken-hearted to see her son behave so badly in public. Being a mother myself, I know I would.

In the meantime, it seems like everywhere you turn, you see these young celebrities and star athletes doing things that are disrespectful, dishonorable, or even scandalous. I can't help but feel terrible for their parents. To be honest, if I behaved like that when I was younger, my parents most likely would have disowned me, since family honor is one of their core values.

I think parenting, and caregiving in general is one "risky business." It's one of those jobs that has unpredictable returns on investment, and could potentially leave you in tremendous emotional pain and/or financial ruin. I'm sure you have seen or known many great parents with terrible children, and vice versa.

As parents, we love our children and wish nothing but the best for them. We try to be the best parents we can be, and strive to instill in them the moral and core values such as love, respect, integrity, honesty, courtesy, work ethic, and compassion. However, in order to keep our sanity and inner peace, we have to understand and accept that no matter how much we love our children, they are separate and independent human beings. Despite our best intention and parenting efforts, our children may or may not turn out the way we would like them to. Our children have free will and their own mind. We cannot control anyone's thoughts, feelings and/or behaviors. All we can control is ourselves. That's why I recommend that you practice *"detached involvement"* when it comes to parenting. It does not mean that you withhold your love, affection, or parenting efforts from your children. It means that you do your best to love and raise them, but be detached from the outcome.

I believe this skill is critical for all parents, caregivers, as well as professionals such as health care providers, teachers, therapists, coaches. When you are in these roles, it's hard not to feel attached and responsible for the outcome of your children, students, patients, or clients. If you are a caregiver, either in your personal or professional life, you need to be especially mindful.

Detached Involvement for Caregivers

Caregiving can be a rough roller coaster ride. There are so many things that are out of your control. You need to make a conscious choice to remain open and flexible, and go with the flow. Don't take it personally when things didn't go as planned, or the person you care for didn't progress as you had hoped. When you have invested so much in a relationship/job, it's only human nature to feel frustrated, disappointed, sad, or even guilty, when things don't turn out the way you hoped for.

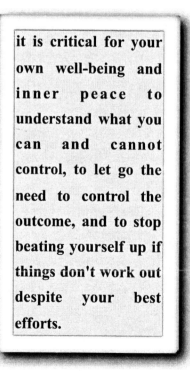

it is critical for your own well-being and inner peace to understand what you can and cannot control, to let go the need to control the outcome, and to stop beating yourself up if things don't work out despite your best efforts.

However, it is critical for your own well-being and inner

peace to understand what you can and cannot control, to let go the need to control the outcome, and to stop beating yourself up if things don't work out despite your best efforts.

When you think about it, this principle applies to practically all relationships and projects. Whenever you go into a relationship or take on a project, you can have the best intention, make the best action plan and try to execute the plan to your best capacity. However, there's always something you cannot control, especially when there is another person involved. Sometimes there are things beyond anyone's control. As a result, things might not turn out according to your plan, despite your best efforts. After all, there are a lot of things beyond your control. As the Chinese proverb goes, "*Man proposes but God disposes.*"

This is not an excuse to blame others for failed relationships and projects. **You are 100% responsible for your own actions, feelings, the choices you make, and the consequences that come as a result. However, you are not responsible for someone else's thoughts, feelings, actions, and the choices they make.**

Practicing detached involvement does not mean that you would withhold your efforts to avoid disappointment. As I wrote earlier, in the case of parenting, you would still try to love and educate your children as best as you could. That's every parent's responsibility. However, you have little control over how your children respond to your teaching, and how they *choose* to live their lives.

My point is, if you have made your best efforts and things didn't work out, there's no point in beating yourself up. It's important to acknowledge and validate your feelings (disappointment, anger, resentment, sadness, for example) Denying your own feelings will only make you feel worse. Instead, find a way to release these feelings, by writing in a journal, meditating, talking to friends, family, your life coach or therapist. **Accept that there's something beyond your control, make peace with the outcome, take the lesson learned, and move on.**

Inner Peace No Matter What

The word crisis in Chinese is made of two characters -- *risk* and *opportunity*. Where there is crisis, there is risk as well as opportunity. Most people, however, only see the risk and suffering during a crisis, and that's exactly what they will experience. When you can see the opportunities (to learn, to grow), the lesson or the blessings in disguise, you will have inner peace under any circumstances.

Self-Coaching Session
Detached Involvement

Whether you are involved in caregiving or any project, take these steps to practice *detached involvement*:

✳ State your intention -- What do you intend to experience in this process?

✳ Create a vision -- What's your desired outcome?

* Create an action plan to achieve your desired outcome -- What's the first step I can take?

* Identify and seek out the support you need -- Who can help you achieve your desired outcome? What resources do you need? How and where can you get such support?

✶ Identify what you can and cannot control in this relationship/project. Awareness is the first step for making changes.

✶ Use daily affirmations to reinforce your intention and vision, and follow your action plan to work on what you can control. Make your best efforts.

＊ When things don't go your way, use affirmations, meditation or prayers to release what you cannot control. Make a conscious choice to let go your need to control the outcome. Ask your Higher Self, the Universe, or God, to take care of what you cannot control. Ask for guidance and inner peace.

＊ Make it your intention to make peace with whatever outcome you receive -- Have faith that everything happens for a reason, and there is a lesson or opportunity to grow in every situation. Look for blessings in disguise. Take the lesson, make peace, and move on.

Key #7

Dare to Connect

"Friendship improves happiness, and abates misery, by doubling our joys, and dividing our grief.
-- Joseph Addison, British Essayist, Poet, Statesman

New Mom on the Block

When my daughter was about nine months old, my husband got a new job in another state. I decided to quit my job in the university and stay home with my daughter. That was our first move as a family. My husband's job later brought us to four states in four calendar years. It was quite an adventure to move with two little kids (under age five) in tow.

Anyway, the first time we moved out of state, we lived in an apartment complex. We didn't know a soul in town. It's not easy making friends in an apartment complex. Being a new mom on the block while making the transition from a full-time career woman to a stay-at-home mom, proved to be very challenging. I felt like I lost my identity and my entire support network. I had no one to talk to, and no one to turn to if I needed help.

Feeling lonely and totally isolated and compounded by the exhaustion of caring for an infant, I started to feel a little depressed. One day I had this terrible thought that if something happened to my daughter and me while my husband was away, nobody would even notice. You know the stories you hear about people dying alone in their apartments and nobody found them until days later. It gave me chills. That's when I decided I must make new friends ASAP. The problem is, all my friends were from school or from work. Since I was not working and not in school any more, I just had no idea where to find new friends.

The next time I went grocery shopping, I happened to glance at the bulletin board, and saw a flyer about Moms Club. Talk about serendipity. Back then, I had never heard of this organization. I figured, since it's a mom's group and I'm a mom, let me check it out.

What a pleasant surprise! I found out they are a national organization, and this local chapter is well-established. They offered many activities and outings for both moms and their young children. The best part is, we found a play group that met once a week. All five moms had college or graduate degrees, and our first-born children were about the same age. My daughter and I thoroughly enjoyed the weekly play group and many outings. The weekly play group was a life-saver, which kept my sanity and affirmed my choice to stay home with my daughter. The moms became close friends. That was 13 years ago when we met. I still keep in touch with some of them.

Connect, Support and Thrive

Fast forward to May 2009. I was invited to speak at a special Mother's Day Tea hosted by the American Cancer Society. The participants were breast cancer survivors, family caregivers and volunteers. Since it was a Mother's Day celebration, I led a discussion on the joy and challenges of motherhood, how to reduce stress and nurture themselves.

> **You need to be aware and acknowledge when you need support from others, and to respect that need. To honor and respect your own needs is an act of self-love and self-compassion. You need to understand and believe that you deserve to love and nurture yourself, at least as much as you love and nurture others.**

We had a lively discussion. Many participants shared their own feelings and experiences. Some stated how much they appreciated hearing other people's experience and knowing that they were not alone. Overall, everyone seemed to perk up by the end of the discussion.

Some recent studies indicated caregivers as the most stressful job, worse than air traffic controllers. Taking care of a loved one with an illness or special needs takes a toll on the caregivers' physical, emotional and financial well-being. When the caregivers neglect their own needs and fail to practice Intensive Self-Care while taking care of their loved ones, they could quickly become burned out.

Caregiving is not for the faint of heart, and it should not be a solo endeavor. If you are a Nurturer (whether you are a mom, family caregiver or medical professional), it's extremely important to have a strong support network. According to a study published in Nurse Education Practice (July 2008), student nurses benefit from sharing their personal feelings and experiences during group reflection sessions. The study participants perceived that these group reflection sessions helped them cope with the overwhelming demands of the clinical environment and altered their perspectives on situations.

More Balance, Less Burnout

If Nurturers are expected to do the full-time jobs of at least two to three people, getting support so you can delegate some of the more routine or especially challenging tasks is simply a good management technique.

Furthermore, getting support is the only way to make any form of life balance within the reach of the average caregivers. Why? Let's do an experiment.

Stand up and try to balance on one foot for as long as you can. How long did you last? I'm guessing not very long. Now, try to balance on one foot, near a wall. Put one finger on the wall for support to help you balance. It's a little easier, isn't it? Now, put your whole hand against the wall for support. I bet it's much easier to balance, and you can last much longer without falling over.

Just as the wall helps you maintain your physical balance, it's important to have a support network of people

> Even with support, you still have to use your own strength to stay standing, but you can stay balanced much longer, without falling over. In the case of caregiving, seeking support is a sign of self-love and intelligent, strategic thinking.

to help you maintain life balance and prevent burnout. Even with support, you still have to use your own strength to stay standing, but you can stay balanced much longer, without falling over. In the case of caregiving, seeking support is a sign of self-love and intelligent, strategic thinking.

Nurturing Reduces Stress

Research has shown that men and women cope with stress differently. Men are likely to isolate themselves, while women are more apt to comfort others and seek help. One fascinating study was the UCLA Friendship Study conducted by Shelley E. Taylor, Ph.D. and her colleague Laura Cousin Klein, Ph.D. The study showed that women react to stressful situations by protecting their young (which the researchers call a "tend" response) and also by seeking out social contact and support from others, especially other women (known as the "befriend" response). In other words, when women are under stress, their natural instinct is to nurture others.

The nurturing ("tend and befriend") behavior causes the release of the chemical oxytocin, a feel good chemical that neutralizes stress, helps you feel calmer, more focused, and more connected to others. Oxytocin is released when friends comfort and help one another and and also when a mother nurses her baby. **Oxytocin**

counteracts the stress hormones adrenaline and cortisol, the same chemicals that cause chronic inflammation, raise blood pressure, lower your immune system, and leave you feeling on edge. So, this natural instinct to nurture others is actually a good survival instinct. Biologically, men will produce the same release of oxytocin when they spend time with loved ones. But their male hormones, especially testosterone, negate some of oxytocin's positive effects.

The Friendship Study demonstrates that women, because they cope with stress by seeking out others, are more likely to stay healthy during times of prolonged stress. They've got the feel good hormone oxytocin on their side. Other studies have shown that social support provides protection against heart disease, mental illness, and many other health conditions, while boosting the immune system. You can say that community equals immunity.

The Gift of Receiving

Everyone knows the gift of giving, but few understand the gift of receiving. It's very gratifying to be able to give and help others, especially when they do appreciate your help, or when you can see how they've benefited from your help. Being altruistic is definitely a virtue; however, some people I know or work with tend to see self-sacrifice as their obligation. These people have the tendency to "over-nurture" at the cost of their own physical or emotional well-being.

The benefits of seeking support from others is obvious, however, not everyone would ask for help when they need it. The problem is that many people equate asking for support as a sign of weakness or inadequacy. For example, a mother or a business owner might reason that she should be able to do it all if she is a capable mother or business owner. On the other hand, some people do not ask for help because they do not want to bother or owe other people favors. As a result, they have the hardest time admitting they need help and/or asking for help. This kind of mentality and behavior will drain you physically and emotionally, and easily lead to burnout.

> **To honor and respect your own needs is an act of self-love and self-compassion. You need to understand and believe that you deserve to love and nurture yourself, at least as much as you love and nurture others.**

The solution, I believe, lies in striking the balance between giving and receiving. It requires heightened self-awareness and self-love. You need to be aware and acknowledge when you need support from others, and to respect that need. To honor and respect your own needs is an act of self-love and self-compassion. You need to understand and believe that you deserve to love and nurture yourself, at least as much as you love and nurture others.

I know, it's easier said than done. I'm often surprised by how uncomfortable some people get about accepting help.

Last Spring, I took my children to Home Depot to buy new plants and top soil for my garden. You know there's always a surplus of guys in that store. Not just any guys -- these are supposedly very strong, capable, DIY type of guys (at least they believe themselves to be, right?). So, on this beautiful sunny afternoon, as I was pulling into the Home Depot parking lot, I saw an old lady standing by her car, attempting to lift the 40-lb bags of top soil into her trunk. She's got to be in her 70s, and looked very frail. I have no idea why she was there all by herself, buying these bags of top soil which she obviously couldn't carry. Perhaps she was counting on some of those strong, capable DIY guys would give her a helping hand. Well, as I parked and got out of my car, I saw a couple big guys walking by her toward the store, but none of them stopped to offer her help. Meanwhile, she was still attempting with no success to lift the first bag of top soil out of the shopping cart.

So, I walked straight to her with my children, and offered to help her. She looked at me for 2 seconds and said, "I don't need your help. I need a man to help me." I guess she had little faith in my 5'3" physique. Or, perhaps she believes that it's a "man's job" to carry the top soil, and I'm not capable or qualified for that. Who knows? In any case, I'm a mom, and I can certainly handle a few bags of top soil.

I looked around, and, as far as I could tell, I did not see any of those strong, capable guys come running to help this poor old lady. Once more, I assured her that I could help her, and she finally decided to let me help her move the bags into her trunk. Then, she made a remark that I thought was bewildering. Instead of saying "thank you", she said, "Now, how am I going to move these into my house? Are you going to follow me home and help me?" I'm not kidding. That's what she said.

As I said good-bye to her and walked toward the store, I pondered on this surreal encounter. On one hand, I was happy that I could help her, and grateful that I was healthy and strong enough to be on the giving end. On the other hand, I have to say, it's kind of disappointing to offer someone help and be turned down. It's also kind of weird that I had to convince the old lady to let me help her, and that she didn't seem to appreciate the assistance even though she obviously needed it. Even though I did help her in the end, it did not feel as gratifying as if she had said yes to me the first time I offered to help.

This got me thinking. Why is it so difficult to accept other's assistance? And, when you know you really need help, does it really matter where it comes from?

Another experience I had years ago was totally different. This time, I was at the receiving end. It was when my children were very little. One day, I had an emergency and my husband was out of town. We had no family nearby at all, and it was hard to get a babysitter on such a short notice. A friend of mine offered to watch my children for a few hours. I couldn't thank her enough after I returned. To

> **When you graciously accept others' offering of assistance, you are not only receiving a gift from them, you are also giving them a precious gift -- an opportunity to receive the gratifying and exhilarating experience of being able to help someone and make a difference in someone's life.**

that she replied, "No, thank YOU for trusting me with your children. It means a lot to me."

I was so moved that I couldn't utter a word. Needless to say, our friendship deepened as a result and I saw her as a true friend.

You see, when you graciously accept others' offering of assistance, you are not only receiving a gift from them, you are also giving them a precious gift -- an opportunity to receive the gratifying and exhilarating experience of being able to help someone and make a difference in someone's life.

If you have helped someone before, you know the feeling I'm talking about. We all want to feel useful and needed. We all want to make a difference. Being able to help makes us feel great about ourselves.

Think about it. **When you turn away an extended helping hand, you are depriving that person an opportunity to feel great about himself/herself.** On the contrary, when you allow someone to give you a helping hand, you are giving them this precious gift of making a difference and feeling great about themselves. That's why I call it the gift of receiving. As a result, you get the help you need, the other person feels great, and it also strengthens your relationship.

Everybody wins.

Step Out and Reach Out

I hope by now you understand the importance of having a solid support network, especially during times of stress. As the saying goes, it takes a village. Back in the old days, most people had their extended families nearby or lived in close-knit communities. There was plenty of emotional support and people ready to lend a helping hand. Nowadays, many people are running themselves ragged because they lack the support network they desperately need. For Nurturers, it's even more critical to have a solid support network. Isolation can easily lead to depression and burnout. As I mentioned before, caregiving is definitely not a solo sport. It's totally unhealthy, not to mention impossible, to try to go it alone.

If you do not have family or friends nearby that can help you, it's time to extend your support network. Instead of waiting for someone to find you and lend you a helping hand, step out and be the first to reach out. You might want to consider building more than one support network. If you are a family caregiver, it's a good idea to connect with other caregivers. There are many local caregiver's coalitions where you can meet with caregivers, healthcare providers, home care agencies and elder care lawyers, etc. There are also all sorts of support groups based on the illness that your loved one has. If you are a stay-at-home mom, join an organization like Moms Club, Mothers & More or Mothers of Preschoolers. Reach out to find friends among the mothers in the park, at your children's school, or online forums. If you are a healthcare professional, you might want to attend your professional association meetings to connect with colleagues in the same field. You can also build a support network around your hobby or your volunteer work. Many people develop deep friendships with others who share the same passion or cause. These are certainly people you could turn to for support.

It's also very important to have respite from your caregiving responsibilities. Who can you reach out to, to take over your duty so you can have a little break from time to time? Can you hire temporary help, even just on an

If you do not have family or friends nearby that can help you, it's time to extend your support network. Instead of waiting for someone to find you and lend you a helping hand, step out and be the first to reach out.

hourly basis? Sometimes you can find help inexpensively. For example, as I wrote earlier in the book, I used to swap babysitting with other moms. Maybe you can find reliable high school students in your own neighborhood who can babysit your child or keep your aging parent company for a couple hours. When you do get someone to help, take advantage of that. Use that time to nurture yourself. Perhaps you want to take a nap, a bubble bath, go out for a manicure or a movie, have coffee with your girlfriend, go to a park or a book store, or get a massage. Whatever nurtures and recharges you, go for it!

And more importantly, don't be afraid to ask for the help you need from your family, spouse, friends, religious leader, neighbors, coworkers, etc. Consider calling me for coaching if you would like to learn how to reduce stress and create more balance, while you continue to take care of others. There are also many government or community-based programs that you might qualify for financial or caregiving assistance.

Remember -- caregiving should never, ever be a solo endeavor. Next time someone offers you a hand, instead of automatically answering, "No thanks, I can handle it," think for a second. Accepting support when you need it is not a sign of weakness. It's an act of self-love. If you could really use the help, then by all means, why not say yes for a change? You will feel much better, and your loved ones will too.

Self-Coaching Session
Dare to Connect

* What type of support network do you have? List the groups, organizations or individuals you can turn to, and what kinds of support they offer.

* What additional support do I need?

* Who can I reach out to for such support? Identify individuals and community groups/programs in your area. Brainstorm with others if you need more ideas.

* What types of respite would I like on a regular basis?

The following questions are for you if you have a hard time accepting other people's help. Next time when you feel the urge to say no to a helping hand, ask yourself these questions:

* Am I saying no because I really don't need any help or because I don't want to "bother" someone else?

* Am I saying no because I'm afraid of being judged as incapable or inadequate?

* Could I use the help? Would this make my life easier?

* What am I trying to accomplish here?

* How important is my long-term health and emotional well-being?

* Could I use someone to share my load so I could take a much-needed break for myself?

* What do I gain by saying yes?

* How does this help my loved ones?

The Choice is Yours

"God, grant me the serenity to accept the things I cannot change, the courage to change the things I can, and the wisdom to know the difference."
-- *Reinhold Niebuhr*

No matter what your circumstances are, no matter what challenges you are facing today, there is always hope. **You can choose to have inner peace, this instant. It's as simple as making a choice, and the choice is yours.**

Yes, it is simple, but not always easy. That's why I wrote this book for you. It is my hope that you find inspiration as well as practical solutions in this book. May it offer peace, hope and inspiration on your journey. More importantly, I hope it inspires you to take action to nurture yourself everyday, while you care for others.

Remember... you are irreplaceable.

About the Author

Hueina Su, MS, BSN, CEC is an internationally recognized expert in helping people find the missing peace in their stressful lives. What sets her apart from other stress management experts is the 5,000 years of ancient Chinese wisdom and culture behind her. Brought up in Taiwan and trained in the U.S., she is known for her wisdom, compassion, and the way she graciously applies her unique blend of Eastern philosophy and western training in solving modern day problems.

Hueina is a keynote speaker, certified professional coach, author, creator of *Rx For Balance*™ coaching program, and the founder & CEO of Beyond Horizon Coaching, a global coaching and training company specializing in providing solutions for stress management, life balance and Intensive Self-Care.

Hueina started her first career as a registered nurse and has more than 20 years of experience in nursing, coaching, counseling, speaking, training, nonprofit management, and small business. Prior to becoming a certified professional coach, she has worked in healthcare, academia, nonprofit, private sector, small business and freelance. Since she has thrived in so many professions and lived in many places, Hueina is extremely adaptable to change and great at reinventing herself. She has lived and traveled extensively in Asia and U.S., which enhances her natural ability to understand, connect and work with people from different backgrounds. Her unique blend of philosophy, training and life experiences are invaluable assets in her coaching ability, and create extraordinary results for her clients.

Brought up in a family with four generations of doctors and nurses, and having been a nurse herself, she knows first-hand the stressful lives they lead. With her extensive personal and professional experiences as a

Nurturer, Hueina understands deeply the challenges that women nurturers face every day. She had experienced and overcome Nurturing Burnout herself as a registered nurse caring for terminal cancer patients, and again as a full-time counselor, commuting 3 hours a day, while caring for her newborn baby. She has since successfully made the transitions from full-time working mother to stay-at-home mom, and now as a professional speaker, author and life coach doing the work she loves. It is her passion and personal mission to empower other Nurturers to practice Intensive Self-Care, create balance and joy, and live the life they truly desire. By changing the lives of female Nurturers, she intends to empower these women as role models for the next generation of women, and impact the lives they will touch for generations to come.

Hueina lives with C. Carey Yang, her husband of 15 years and their two beautiful children in New Jersey, U.S.A. In her spare time, she enjoys photography, reading, writing, music, martial arts training, fencing, yoga, movies, travel, hanging out with friends and family, volunteering at her children's schools and charity. She holds a Black Belt in Tae Kwon Do, has competed and won multiple gold medals in Tae Kwon Do, Kung Fu and Tai Chi Sword, in NJ state and regional tournaments. One of her personal goals is to become a grandma with lots of inspiring and adventurous stories to tell. She is working on that every day.

Additional Resources

www.RxForBalance.com -- Sign up for a **FREE Intensive Self-Care Kit** and get information about *Rx for Balance*™ coaching & training program, keynotes, Teleclass and other resources.

www.HueinaSu.com -- The official website of Hueina Su with her keynote speaking & coaching information, videos as well as her blog. Get insider scoop on her upcoming book *Invisible Chaos*.

www.CoachingOasis.com -- Get on an one-year self-discovery life makeover journey with Hueina Su as your personal mentor, as she guides you toward greater success, happiness, confidence and fulfillment in every area of your life.

www.TrueHealingOils.com -- Therapeutic-grade essential oils for optimal stress relief, physical and emotional healing. These essential oils are amazing tools for Intensive Self-Care and personal transformation. Check out the great educational information on holistic health for you and your family.

Other Products from Hueina Su

Intensive Care for the Nurturer's Soul –
7 Keys to Nurture Yourself While Caring for Others

A Must Read interactive guidebook for caregivers, parents, healthcare professionals and all nurturers.

Book - $19.99
Qty. ....

The Balancing Act
Time Management for Busy Professionals

Learn effective time management strategies for maximum productivity and minimum stress.

CD - $19.99
Qty. ....

Effortless Decision Making
Strategies for the Indecisive

Learn powerful tips and tools to help you make up your mind so you can move forward.

CD - $19.99
Qty. ....

Changing Lanes
Secrets of Successful Midlife Career Change

Learn about job satisfaction myths, common career change mistakes, overcoming "the age thing" and proactive steps to make a successful midlife career change.

CD - $19.99
Qty. ....

Learn to Say NO, So You Can
Say YES to Your Life

A Prescription for Stress-Free Living

Learn to Say NO, So You can
say YES to Your Life

Learn the critical 7-step process to turn negative emotion into
positive actions when you say no in order to live a balanced life.

CD - $19.99
Qty. _____

A Prescription for Stress-Free Living

Learn the root cause of stress, the signs of stress and burnout, and
the powerful 3-prong approach to relieve chronic stress, create
more joy and balance in very area of your life.

CD - $19.99
Qty. _____

Rx *for* Balance	Phone: (973) 664-0446	Fax: (866) 903-1442

Name _____

Tel # _____

Email _____

Company _____

Address _____

City _____ State _____ Zip _____

Payment by: □Visa □Mastercard □Amex □Discover

Credit Card # _____ Exp. Date _____
3 Digit Code _____

Print Name as it Appears on Card_____

Signature_____Date_____

Shipping & Handling:
$5 for the first item
$1 for each additional item

Subtotal _____

S&H _____

Total _____

3 Ways to Order:
1. Fax 24 Hours a Day (866) 903-1422
2. Call 1-973-664-0446
3. Mail to: Hueina Su
   4 Dogwood Drive, Denville, NJ 07834

Ask about Group Order Discount

Do you know of any organization (Corp/Assn/College) that may be interested in having Hueina Su as a Guest Speaker?

Name _____ Organization _____

Email _____ Tel # _____ -_____

* Special discounts are available on quantity purchases by corporations, nonprofit, universities, professional associations, and others. For more information, please contact customer service at
www.RxForBalance.com.
Phone: (973) 664-0446
Fax: (866) 903-1442